W9-AMA-645

CULTURES OF THE WORLD

MONGOLIA

Guek-Cheng Pang

MARSHALL CAVENDISH
New York • London • Sydney

Reference edition published 1999 by
Marshall Cavendish Corporation
99 White Plains Road
Tarrytown
New York 10591

© Times Editions Pte Ltd 1999

Originated and designed by
Times Books International, an imprint of
Times Editions Pte Ltd

Printed in Malaysia

Library of Congress Cataloging-in-Publication Data:

Pang, Guek-Cheng.
    Mongolia / Guek-Cheng Pang.
        p. cm.—(Cultures of the World)
    Includes bibliographical references and index.
    Summary: Describes the geography, history, government,
economy, people, lifestyle, religion, language, arts, leisure,
festivals, and food of Mongolia.
    ISBN 0-7614-0954-8
    1. Mongolia—Juvenile literature. [1. Mongolia.]
I. Title. II. Series.
DS798.C44   1999
951'.7—dc21   98–31897
                    CIP
                    AC

INTRODUCTION

WHEN WE THINK OF THE MONGOLS, the picture that comes to mind is that of the fierce and ruthless warriors who swept out of Central Asia in the 12th and 13th centuries, cutting a bloody swath across the land and creating the Mongol empire. We think of Marco Polo, the Italian adventurer who traveled east to China and brought back incredible tales of Kublai Khan's court. We see a nomadic people living a relatively simple life, riding horses, tending to animals, living in tents. We think of an undeveloped nation of people under communist rule, cut off from the modern world.

Mongolia has been all these things. But today, Mongolia is a land of people rich in culture, proud of their history, striving to overcome the strictures of more than six decades of communism. Mongolians are a people in transition, rediscovering their heroes and traditions, and finding a place for themselves in today's changing world.

CONTENTS

A Shamanist marker in the mountains.

CONTENTS

A Mongolian child drinking tea.

GEOGRAPHY

LOOK AT A MAP of Asia, and you will find Mongolia in Central Asia between two big and powerful countries, Russia and China. Mongolia is shaped like a pair of smiling lips. To the north Mongolia shares a border of more than 2,000 miles (3,220 km) with the Siberian part of Russia. In the south is a 3,000-mile (4,830 km) border with China. To the east lies Manchuria, and to the west, the Xinjiang Uighur Autonomous Region.

Mongolia is an independent country, not to be confused with Inner Mongolia in north China. The people of the two regions share a similar culture, however.

Mongolia is slightly larger than Alaska, with an area of 604,000 square miles (1,565,000 square km). The population is just over 2.3 million, so there are fewer than three people per square mile (less than one person per square km).

Opposite and left: **A view of Ulaanbaatar, the capital of Mongolia, and** *ger* **("GUHR"), or tent settlements in the suburbs.**

The Altai mountains in western Mongolia.

The forestry management program ensures that logging does not worsen soil erosion and that reforestation is carried out by replanting trees.

HIGH, DRY, AND COLD

Mongolia has a high average altitude of 5,000 feet (1,523 m). Mountainous areas higher than 10,000 feet (3,047 m) form less than 5% of the total land area. About 40% of the country lies between 3,000 feet (914 m) and 10,000 feet (3,047 m) above sea level. Even the lowest part, the Höh Nuur depression in the east, is 1,746 feet (532 m) above sea level. The highest areas are in western, northern, and central Mongolia, and the lower elevations are in the east and south.

There are three major mountain ranges. The Altai range in the west and southwest is the largest and highest mountain range in the country. The highest point is the Hüyten peak (Nayramädlïn), which rises to 15,272 feet (4,653 m) above sea level, in the Tavan Bogd mountain group of the Altai range. Much of this range is snow-covered all year round.

The other two mountain ranges in Mongolia are the more heavily forested Hangai and Hentii ranges in north-central and northwestern Mongolia. The wetter mountain slopes of the Hangai and Hentii are forested with cedar, larch, birch, pine, and fir. Above the tree line are alpine meadows with mosses and lichens that bloom in the spring. On the northern part of the Hangai mountains are a number of extinct volcanoes and volcanic lakes. Wild sheep, ibex, and gazelles roam the mountains. The rare snow leopard lives in the high mountains along the border with Russia.

Mountain climbers from all over the world visit Mongolia to climb the mountains, especially the Altai range. The mountain climbing season begins in early July and ends in August.

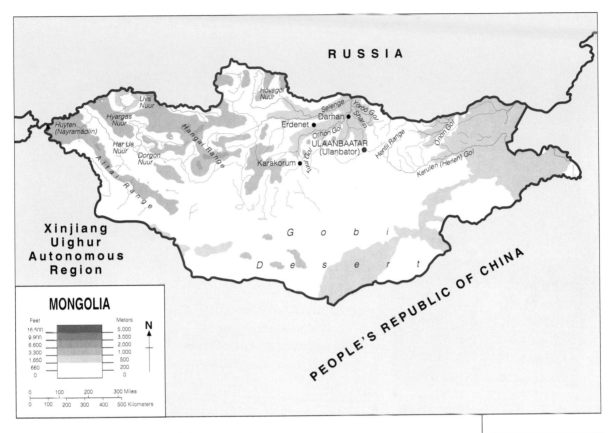

RUSSIA

Hovsgol
Nuur

Uvs
Nuur

Hyargas
Nuur

Huyten
(Nayramädlin)

Selenge
Yorōō Gol
Darhan
Erdenet
Orhon Gol
Shariin
Har Us
Nuur

Dorgon
Nuur

ULAANBAATAR
(Ulanbator)

Karakorum

Hentii Range

Onon Gol

Kerulen (Herlen) Gol

Xinjiang
Uighur
Autonomous
Region

G   o   b   i

D   e   s   e   r   t

PEOPLE'S REPUBLIC OF CHINA

MONGOLIA

Feet	Meters
16,500	5,000
9,900	3,000
6,600	2,000
3,300	1,000
1,650	500
660	200
0	0

N

0   100   200   300 Miles
0 100 200 300 400 500 Kilometers

THE GOBI DESERT

In the south lies the famous Gobi Desert, which Mongolia shares with China. The world's coldest, northernmost desert covers more than 500,000 square miles (1,295,000 square km). The Gobi is windswept and nearly treeless. Only 5% of it is sand dunes while the rest is mostly dry, rocky, and sandy soil. The Gobi is actually a plateau of rolling gravel plains, with occasional low ranges and isolated hills. It rises from 3,000 feet (914 m) in the east to 5,000 feet (1,523 m) in the west, where it meets the Altai mountains. The desert vegetation is grass and scrub. People and livestock here rely on water from small, shallow lakes and wells.

Caravan routes have crisscrossed the Gobi since ancient times. Marco Polo, his father, and his uncle were the first Europeans to cross the desert around A.D. 1275. The Gobi is a famous repository of fossils, especially of the Late Cretaceous period.

The 13 nature reserves in Mongolia are an important part of the government's efforts to preserve the environment. The largest is the Great Gobi Reserve. The rare Gobi bear is the world's only desert bear.

DINOSAUR LAND

In 1918 naturalist, adventurer, and fossil-hunter Roy Chapman Andrews (1884–1960) drove across the Gobi Desert and was convinced he had found the Garden of Eden. Andrews worked at the American Museum of Natural History in New York City. He was director of the museum from 1935 to 1942. In 1922, 1923, and 1925, he returned to the Gobi with the museum's first scientific expedition, hoping to find the bones of early humans to confirm the theory that *homo sapiens* had evolved in high, dry climates such as that of Central Asia. Instead, he discovered that the Gobi was a great repository of dinosaur remains. Andrews discovered the first dinosaur eggs at a time when scientists were not even sure that dinosaurs laid eggs. In *On the Trail of Ancient Man*, Andrews wrote, "We realized we were looking at the first dinosaur eggs ever seen by a human being.... The elongated shape of the eggs was distinctly reptilian." The eggs (like those of the protoceratops fossil in the picture above) were found in the area of the Gobi called Ulan Usu, which Andrews called the "Flaming Red Cliffs" because of the area's sheer red-rock cliffs, buttes, and gullies.

Other expeditions have discovered fossilized animals and plants from the early Paleozoic and Mesozoic, when this area was covered by great seas and lakes. The Gobi has yielded the skeletons of previously unknown dinosaurs, as well as the tiny skulls of some of the earliest known mammals. The desert fossil beds are extensive and extremely well preserved because of the dry desert climate.

In the 1960s a Mongolian-Polish scientific team discovered skeletons of a velociraptor and a protoceratops that were killed by a violent sandstorm as they were trying to kill each other. In 1993 a team from the American Museum of Natural History and the Mongolian Academy of Sciences discovered an oviraptor fossil seated on a clutch of eggs, the first evidence of a dinosaur showing parental care. Dinosaur exhibits can be seen in the Ulaanbaatar Museum of Natural History.

THE STEPPES

The steppes or grasslands cover mainly the eastern part of the country. The vegetation here is made up of all varieties of feather grass common to the steppes of Central Asia. These are the grasses that sustain the millions of sheep, horses, goats, cattle, and other livestock that are the mainstay of the Mongolian economy. Herds of antelope also roam these grasslands.

In the springtime, the countryside changes from the harsh look it has most of the year. It begins to turn a vivid green as everything comes alive, and some hills are carpeted in a tapestry of bright yellow, purple, pale violet, and crimson. Millions of wildflowers burst into bloom to make the most of the short growing season.

Young boys enjoying a ride in the springtime.

The Orhon River in north central Mongolia. Mongolia's rivers and lakes teem with many species of fish including the world's largest salmonid, which weighs more than 100 pounds (45 kg).

Mongolians are being taught that, with limited water resources, the rivers and lakes must be protected and the dumping of sewage and waste controlled.

RIVERS AND LAKES

Mongolia is a dry land. Total rainfall during the year is 4 inches (10 cm) in the desert and 14 inches (36 cm) in the north. Thus the many rivers, lakes, and glaciers are an important source of water.

Over 1,200 rivers drain in one of three directions—north into the Arctic Ocean, east into the Pacific Ocean, or south into the desert. The longest rivers are the Selenge, one of the rivers flowing into Lake Baikal in Russia, the Orhon, a tributary of the Selenge, and the Tuul. Their source is in the Hangai range. The Herlen and Onon rivers originate in the Hentii range. There are about 200 glaciers, found in the Altai mountains alone.

Mongolia has more than 4,000 lakes. Many are small, with an average surface area of 2 square miles (5 square km), but the total area of all the lakes is just over 1% of Mongolia's land area. Many lakes were formed by glacial and volcanic activity and are concentrated between the Altai and the Hangai ranges. The Uvs is a saltwater lake and the largest in Mongolia. The Hövsgöl is the deepest lake in Mongolia and Central Asia.

LONG, COLD WINTERS

Mongolia lies between latitudes 50°N and 42°N, in the same belt as the Ukraine, Romania, Hungary, Austria, and northern United States. The country is totally landlocked; the nearest sea is the Yellow Sea, about 435 miles (700 km) to the east.

Mongolia has a continental climate characterized by extreme temperature changes. From November to March average temperatures are below freezing. The coldest month is usually January, when temperatures can drop to as low as –62°F (–52°C).

In the summer, the hottest month is usually July, when temperatures range from 68°F (20°C) in the northern regions to about 86°F (30°C) in the south. Temperature changes of as much as 35–55°F (2–13°C) can occur in one day.

"… the real summer lasts only from May till August. Then, the valleys are like an exquisite garden and the woods are ablaze with color. Bluebells, their stalks bending under the weight of blossoms, clothe every hillside in a glorious azure dress bespangled with yellow roses, daisies, and forget-me-nots."

—*Roy Chapman Andrews in* Across Mongolian Plains

Snow settles on the *ger* roofs in a district of Ulaanbaatar.

A herdsman moves his flock of animals beneath the cloudless blue sky.

THE IMMORTAL BLUE SKY

The distance from the sea and the fact that any moisture-laden winds from the east encounter a mountain range ensure that the winds that blow over Mongolia are dry. Little rain falls in Mongolia, although the mountainous regions of the north are wetter than the south. The rainy season is between May and September.

The lack of humidity means that on most days the sun shines brightly from a blue and often cloudless sky. Mongolians boast that they enjoy as many as 250 sunny days a year. Traditional Mongolians believe the immense blue sky is the Supreme God, called *Tengri* ("TENG-ri"). They also say that blue is a lucky color.

Mongolia is also known as the land of winds because of the sharp winds that blow in the springtime and often become storms.

DISTINCTIVE FAUNA

The Asian or Bactrian camels of Mongolia are part of the remaining 700,000 Asian camels in the world. These camels have two humps and are smaller than the Arabian camel or dromedary. They graze on the poor desert grasses and can live for three months on water alone.

The Mongol horse is small, has a thick well-muscled neck, and a bulky head. It is remarkably tough and can survive harsh winters. It resembles Przewalski's horse, a species of wild horse that once roamed the Gobi Desert and the steppes and became extinct in the wild in 1970. In 1994, 19 Przewalski's horses from zoos were released back into the wild.

Mongolia is also a resting point for migratory birds that fly from the northern parts of the Asian continent to the warmer shores of the Indian and Pacific oceans in the winter. These are mainly waterfowl and other birds that live near water.

Above: **A fledgling eagle in its nest. Mongolia is home to the golden eagle and condor, as well as magpies, jays, wood-peckers, goshawks, and grouse.**

Left: **Herds of Mongol horses grazing on the steppes.**

SMALL TOWN MONGOLIA

Most Mongolians live in the countryside, in small towns. The facilities usually include concrete municipal office buildings, a central square, a dilapidated power station, and a fuel dump on the outskirts for the trucks passing by. Residents live in concrete apartment buildings or in *ger*, traditional structures made of a wooden frame covered with layers of felt. A wooden fence surrounds each *ger* so that it can be assigned a house number and the town administration can provide the residents with postal and other services. Sometimes there are also communities of several hundred *ger*, laid out in blocks separated by roads.

A child near his *ger* in the middle of concrete apartment buildings.

Ulaanbaatar, the capital, was founded in 1639, when it was named Urga. The name changed many times before becoming Ulaanbaatar ("Red Hero") in 1924. It was once a center of Buddhism and the residence of the Bogdo Khan, a religious leader. The city lies in the Tuul river valley of north-central Mongolia. It is the political, cultural, economic, and industrial center of the country, and the only big city in terms of population; about a quarter of the entire Mongolian population lives here.

Darhan, north of the capital, is the second largest city with about 90,000 residents. It is an industrial center built from the ground up in 1961 in an area rich in limestone, sand, clay, marble, and coal—materials important in construction. Darhan is the center of the construction industry and also produces consumer goods and foodstuffs.

Erdenet lies in the north, between the Selenge and Orhon rivers. The town grew around an ore-dressing plant that was built in 1974. The plant is Asia's largest copper-molybdenum, ore-dressing plant, with an annual output of 16 million tons (14.5 million metric tonnes).

HISTORY

WARLIKE, SAVAGE, AND BRUTAL, the Mongols rode out of the heart of Asia in the 13th century and subjugated the nations in their path, from Central Asia to the banks of the Danube River. China came under Mongol domination for more than a century, Russia for more than two centuries.

NOMADIC TRIBES

The steppes of Central Asia were inhabited by nomadic tribes, probably of Turkic, Tataric, or Ugrian origin, before the Mongolian nation emerged. The Chinese emperor Shi Huang Di built the Great Wall of China to keep out these marauding tribes, specifically the Xiung-nu, believed to be related to the Huns, another fierce group of conquerors.

In 209 B.C., the Huns established the first state in Central Asia. The Huns later split into two groups. One went west, moving from the steppes north of the Caspian Sea to the Roman empire in the 4th and 5th centuries. The other group established the Han and Xia states, south of the Great Wall.

From the 7th to the 10th century, nomadic people, including the Avars, Turks, Uighur, Tang, and Kitan, successively rose to power, became fragmented, and moved westward, or became integrated with the Chinese.

The Mongols were a small group of nomadic people who moved from place to place with the seasons. They fought each other and formed alliances when defeated in battle or when it was in their best interests to do so. These alliances would change according to the strengths of the different clans.

Above: **A teacher takes her young charges to see a mural at the monument honoring Soviet soldiers.**

Opposite: **A portrait of Lenin looks out over Mongolian soldiers on parade.**

19

The rise of the Mongol people began in the time of Chinggis Khan (1167–1227, commonly known as Genghis Khan), who was the first ruler of Mongolia to unite the tribes of Central Asia. Before he became ruler, his name was Temujin. He inherited the leadership of his clan from his father and gained power by conquering and making alliances with the other clans.

In 1206, at a great assembly of all the tribes, Temujin was proclaimed Chinggis Khan, meaning "strong ruler," and all the clans agreed to adopt the name "Mongol."

THE MONGOL EMPIRE

Chinggis began to build his empire in 1209 with a campaign against the southern kingdom of Xi Xia, ruled by the Tanguts. They controlled oases along the Silk Road linking China with Rome. Caravans, including those of the Mongols, traveled this route carrying all kinds of goods and were heavily taxed. Defeated in 1210, Xi Xia became Mongolia's first vassal state.

A statue of Chinggis Khan.

Next to be conquered was the Jin empire, which was already suffering from internal troubles. Other conquests soon followed; the Mongols expanded west, defeating the Kara-Khitai empire west of the Altai mountains, and the cities of Samarkand, Bukhara, Merv, and Herat belonging to the Muslim empire of Khwarizm. The Mongols entered Russian territory and threatened to conquer the Russian principalities of Kiev, Chernigov, Galicia, Rostov, and Suzdal, before deciding to return to their homeland in Central Asia.

THE MONGOL WAR MACHINE

The Mongol cavalryman was lightly clad in leather, giving him greater agility than the more heavily armored European knight. He carried a small leather shield on his left arm for protection. His weapons included a lance, a bow with a quiver of arrows, a saber, and a dagger. He had arrows for different purposes, some with heads designed solely for killing that whistled when released to terrify the enemy, and others that both whistled and wounded the enemy. The Mongol soldier was trained to shoot while riding at full gallop, and was equally adept at hitting targets in front as well as behind him.

A herd of fresh horses was always kept ready and each cavalryman had a reserve of up to four remounts. As basic training, soldiers joined an annual game hunt in which wild animals were chased into a given area and shot by horsemen. Each soldier was given only one arrow to kill the animal of his choice.

Bombardiers with mangonels, or giant catapults, supported the cavalry. When laying siege to a city, Mongols used these to hurl stones, rocks, trees, and even animal corpses, to breach the walls.

As the young Temujin began to gather followers and grew in power, one of the tribes he defeated and mercilessly exterminated were the Tatars who had killed his father. The Europeans confused the name Tatars with the similar-sounding Tartarus, a region of hell. They called the Mongols by that name because they appeared to be devils incarnate.

Many chose to submit rather than be killed, paid taxes, and provided men to the army, adding to Mongol military strength. Chinese, Turks, Persians, Armenians, Georgians, and others fought beside Mongol soldiers. Skilled craftsmen, musicians, and administrators were taken prisoner to serve the khan. Millions were subjugated. The wars of this period caused great destruction but unified Asian and European tribes and for a very long time brought Eastern and Western civilizations together.

Chinggis died in 1227, age 60, of a fall from a horse. By 1280, the Mongol empire built by Chinggis, his sons Jochi, Chaghatai, Ogodei, and Tolui, and his grandsons stretched over all Asia almost to the Mediterranean Sea. But the empire soon began to break down into smaller, independent fiefdoms ruled by different branches of the family.

Mongol soldiers showing off their skills.

SONS OF CHINGGIS

After Chinggis' death in 1227, Ogodei was chosen to be the Great Khan. Ogodei continued to expand the empire. He subdued Xi Xia, which had rebelled, continued to conquer the rich Song empire, and sent a new army to the west.

He made Karakorum his capital, building it from a simple base camp into a great walled city with the help of skilled, captive craftsmen. News of its splendors spread to the West. In 1238 the Mongols under Batu, Jochi's son, attacked and defeated Russia, a few principalities at the time, and moved on to Poland and Hungary in 1241. The Mongols then crossed into Austria. When they almost reached Vienna, news of Ogodei's death in 1242 arrived from Karakorum, and they withdrew.

In the following years, there was a great power struggle between Batu and his cousin Guyuk, Ogodei's son. Batu remained in southern Russia where he established his own capital, Sarai, and ruled his fiefdom known as the Golden Horde. Power then passed to the sons of Tolui.

Mongke, Tolui's eldest son, was enthroned in 1251, and with his brother, Kublai, renewed the assault against the Song. Another brother, Hulagu, attacked Baghdad, the heart of the Muslim world. The caliph (ruler) and his family were killed, and the Muslim empire became the Ilkhanate (subordinate khanate), ruled by Hulagu. His lands stretched from present-day Pakistan to Turkey. After Mongke died in 1259, there was a power struggle between Kublai, still battling the Song, and Arigh Boke, the youngest brother, in Karakorum. Kublai returned to Mongolia and fought Arigh Boke, winning power in 1264. He proclaimed himself Great Khan. The great Mongol empire had by this time broken into fiefdoms.

Kublai had spent much time in northern China (modern Inner Mongolia), and established a capital at Shangdu. He set himself the task of developing and unifying China. He founded the Yuan dynasty and moved his capital to the more centrally located Dadu (present-day Beijing). He encouraged trade, improved Chinese agriculture, advanced the study of the sciences, and developed a written script for the Mongol language. In 1279 he finally defeated the Song empire and united north and south China. He attempted to invade Japan in 1274 and 1281, and Java in Southeast Asia in 1292, without success. Kublai Khan died in 1294 at the age of 79.

An engraving of Kublai Khan.

The Mongols' 89-year rule of China, as the Yuan dynasty, ended in 1368, when the Chinese—tired of ever-increasing taxes and the corruption of officials—rebelled. The Mongols were forced back to Mongolia by the succeeding Ming dynasty, whose rulers rebuilt the Great Wall of China to ensure that the Mongols and other marauding tribes were kept out.

MONGOL DECLINE

After their defeat in China, the Mongols retreated to their homeland. Over the next few centuries the unity that had created their great empire dissolved as the various tribes jostled for power.

Meanwhile, the Mongols were caught between Russia and China. The Manchus of northeast China had assumed power in China and formed the Qing dynasty (1644–1911). Russia and China were making alliances and rapidly expanding their influence in the area. From the 14th century until Mongolia became a people's republic in the early 20th century, events in both Russia and China had a significant impact on Mongolia.

From the 14th to the 17th centuries, the Mongol tribes fought among themselves. The Oirads in the west split with the Khalkhas in the east. Later, these two big groups splintered into smaller tribes that continued intertribal fighting, allowing the Chinese to invade and control them. The various tribes became vassals of China. In the late 16th century Buddhism took hold in Mongolia. Gombordorji Zanabazar (1635–1723), the young son of a wealthy prince, was proclaimed leader of the Buddhists, the Jebtsundamba Khutuktu or reincarnate lama, in 1641.

During the 1750s, the Manchus decided for administrative purposes to divide Mongolia into northern and southern regions. The southern provinces were known as Inner Mongolia and were practically a part of China. The northern provinces were known as Outer Mongolia.

Chinese traders and moneylenders played a major role in Mongolian society. The Mongolians came increasingly under debt to the Manchus, paid high taxes, and were always resentful of being dominated by them. So when the Manchus were overthrown in 1911, it was an opportunity for Outer Mongolia, with Russia's support, to declare independence.

GOD-KING AND DIVINE PLANS

The Mongolian revolt was led by the eighth Jebtsundamba Khutuktu who ruled Mongolia with the consent of the Manchus. He was called the Bogdo Khan, champion of God and supporter of civilization, and revered as a God-King uniting state and religion. He backed Mongolian nationalistic ambitions with the aim of reuniting Mongolia once more. He even tried to regain the territory of Inner Mongolia from China. He was also a drunk and a womanizer who supported his degenerate lifestyle by selling his blessings to the people.

The Winter Palace of the Bogdo Khan is now a museum.

In 1915, with Russian support, Mongolia was able to get China to sign a treaty involving all three countries in which the Chinese were forced to recognize Outer Mongolia's independence while retaining control of Inner Mongolia. But in 1919 Chinese troops invaded Mongolia and imprisoned the Bogdo Khan. Russia, caught in the upheaval of the Russian Revolution and World War I, was unable to help.

This time, deliverance from the Chinese came through a strange and colorful figure, Baron Roman Feodorovich von Ungern-Sternberg, also known as the Mad Baron, a Russian tsarist general who had escaped the revolution in Russia. He believed he was part of a divine plan to liberate Mongolia. In 1921, with an army of opportunists, including Russians, Mongolians, Tibetans, and Poles, the Baron attacked Urga, routed the Chinese army, and rescued the Bogdo Khan.

Having helped Mongolia, the Mad Baron decided that the divine plan called for him to save Russia from the communists. This gave Russia an excuse to intervene in Mongolian affairs.

The Russian Revolution of October 1917 saw the communist Bolshevik forces fighting against the White Russian army of the tsar. The Bolsheviks helped the Mongolian nationalists in their fight for independence.

A REVOLUTION TAKES PLACE

Meanwhile, nationalistic feelings were on the rise in Mongolia. People were increasingly opposed to the Chinese invaders as well as the Mad Baron and his White Russian army, which was turning out to be an army of occupation. When the Chinese invaded Mongolia in 1919, a group of Mongolian nationalists fled across the border to Siberia and formed the Mongolian People's Revolutionary Party. Among them were the revolutionary leaders Damdin Sukhebaatar and Horlyn Choibalsan.

When the Mad Baron drove out the Chinese in February 1921 and declared an independent Mongolia, the revolutionaries' task became twice as difficult. Mongolia had to be freed first from the Chinese and then from the White Russian army. But in March 1921, with the backing of socialist Russia, which in 1917 had undergone a revolution bringing down the tsar, Sukhebaatar crossed the border and drove out both the Chinese and the White Russians and went on to capture Urga.

Independence was declared on July 11, 1921. The Bogdo Khan was allowed to remain as head of state, making Mongolia a republican monarchy from 1921 to 1924. When he died in 1924 there was no attempt to find a successor.

In 1924 the Mongolian People's Republic was declared. This communist, Soviet-style republic with a one-party system remained in power until 1990.

The country once again was closed to the outside world. Josef Stalin's policies in Russia had far-reaching effects on Mongolia; there were campaigns of political terror, purges, arrests, and an attack against Mongolian feudal culture. In 1929, when Stalin launched the policy of collectivization, Mongolia was expected to do the same. Hundreds of Russian advisors and technicians were brought in to help.

DAMDIN SUKHEBAATAR

Damdin Sukhebaatar (1893–1923)—Sukhebaatar means "ax hero"—was conscripted into the Mongolian army when he was 19. He was intelligent and a natural leader, and soon became a junior noncommissioned officer. After distinguishing himself in border clashes with the Chinese, he was promoted to senior NCO.

When the Chinese invaded Mongolia in 1919, he joined a small group of like-minded army friends to plan a revolution. With the help of Russian agents, Sukhebaatar's group and another group led by Horlyn Choibalsan fled to Siberia, where they received military training from the Russians. When Baron von Ungern-Sternberg drove out the Chinese, Sukhebaatar and his followers moved to Hiagt (now Troitskosavsk) on the Russian border and formed the Mongolian People's Revolutionary Party.

In March 1921, Sukhebaatar crossed the border and drove the Chinese out of the town of Amgalanbaatar. He made it a provisional capital, renaming it Altanbulag.

The Baron attacked the revolutionary government. Sukhebaatar, Choibalsan, and the Russian army repulsed this attack, captured the capital city of Urga and proclaimed the independence of Mongolia on July 11, 1921.

Sukhebaatar died suddenly and mysteriously at age 30 in 1923. He is celebrated as Mongolia's great revolutionary hero. His body lies in a mausoleum in Sukhebaatar Square, the main square of Ulaanbaatar. A statue of him astride a horse stands in his honor.

These words are engraved at the base of the statue of Sukhebaatar in Ulaanbaatar: "If we, all the people, are united in common effort and common will, there can be nothing in the world that we cannot achieve, that we will not have learned, or failed to do."

COMMUNIST MONGOLIA

Stalin's instrument in Mongolia was Marshal Choibalsan, one of the founders of the Mongolian People's Revolutionary Party, who controlled the government, army, and secret police. Mongolian herders were divided into rich and poor. Anyone with more than 200 sheep was considered rich, and his animals were seized and given to the poor. Property was appropriated from the monasteries; thousands of lamas were killed and hundreds of temples and monasteries destroyed. Chinese businessmen were expelled from the country.

In 1931 Japan invaded Manchuria and threatened to take over Mongolia. But joint Soviet-Mongolian forces met the threat successfully. Subsequently Russia and China signed an anti-Japanese treaty that also recognized Mongolia's independence.

When Choibalsan died in 1952, Yumjaagiyn Tsedenbal became president. During his long tenure (1952–84), he promoted Russian culture. People had to speak Russian, schools and universities taught in Russian, and people wore Western suits instead of the *del* ("DEHL"), the traditional Mongolian dress. Intellectuals were persecuted for having independent views. Tsedenbal was ousted in 1984.

DEMOCRATIC CHANGES

In the late 1980s, the Soviet Union implemented *perestroika* ("peh-res-TROY-ka") and *glasnost* ("GLAHS-nost"), policies calling for restructuring the economy and greater openness in political affairs. Jambyn Batmönh, who succeeded Tsedenbal, reorganized the government and decentralized the economy. In July 1990 the first free elections were held.

Opposite: **Josef Stalin's statue before it was torn down in 1990, when US Secretary of State James Baker visited Mongolia.**

CHRONOLOGY

1162 Temujin is born.
1206 Temujin is proclaimed Chinggis Khan at a great assembly.
1209 Chinggis launches an attack on Xi Xia in China.
1227 Chinggis Khan dies.
1229 Ogodei is proclaimed Khan.
1279 Kublai Khan completes conquest of China.
1294 Kublai Khan dies.
1400 Breakdown of the Mongol empire, civil war in Mongolia.
1641 Zanabazar is proclaimed leader of the Buddhists in Mongolia.
1911 Mongolia declares independence from China.
1915 Russia, China, and Mongolia sign a treaty giving Mongolia limited autonomy.
1919 Mongolia is reincorporated into China.
1921 Sukhebaatar proclaims Mongolia's independence after defeating Chinese troops.
1924 Mongolian People's Republic is declared after the death of the Bogdo Khan.
1990 The people hold pro-democracy protests.
1992 A new constitution is announced.
1996 The Mongolian Democratic Alliance wins the June election.

GOVERNMENT

MONGOLIA IS IN A STATE OF TRANSITION. It was a feudal society for much of its pre-modern history and entered the 20th century as a socialist state. For more than 65 years of political history, it was a communist state under the influence of the Soviet Union and cut off from the rest of the world. When the dismantling of communism took place in the Soviet Union and other East European countries, and student protests occurred in China, Mongolians also demonstrated for change. Today Mongolia embraces a democratic system of government and is learning to take its place in the world of nations.

REINS OF POWER

Mongolia has a parliamentary government. The State Great Hural ("HOO-rahl"), or parliament, is the highest legislature in the land. The State Great

After Mongolia declared independence in 1921, the first noncommunist country to give it recognition was India, in 1955. Mongolia became a member of the United Nations in 1961 and was given diplomatic recognition by the United Kingdom and other West European and developing countries in 1963. The United States recognized Mongolia in 1987.

Left: **Mongolians proudly display their national flag.**

Opposite: **The national emblem of Mongolia.**

Hural, a unicameral body, has 76 members. It appoints the prime minister and members of his cabinet, which is the highest executive body of the state and ensures all policies of the State Great Hural are implemented. It also oversees the activities of the smaller local governments.

The Supreme Court, which includes the chief justice and his judges, is the highest judicial authority in the land. Judges are elected by the State Great Hural for a four-year term.

The Mongolian legal system is a blend of Russian, Chinese, and Turkish law. Civil law, which is closely modeled on the Russian system, governs relations between people, protecting their rights and the rights of the family. Civil and criminal cases are settled in the people's district courts and provincial courts.

The Great Hural building behind the mausoleum of Sukhebaatar.

LOCAL ADMINISTRATION

In order to govern Mongolia's large area, the country is divided into 21 administrative regions: 18 *aimag* ("AI-mug"), or provinces, and the three municipalities of Ulaanbaatar, Darhan, and Erdenet. The largest *aimag* is the Gobi Desert region of Umnugov. It has 63,690 square miles (165,000 square km) of land, a very rigorous climate, and is the most sparsely populated, with only 45,800 people.

Each *aimag* is divided into smaller districts, of which there are 298 in Mongolia. The *aimag* are governed by small legislative organizations called *hural*. Deputies or representatives of the people are elected to the *hural* for three-year terms.

POLITICAL UPHEAVAL

Toward the end of the 1980s, the changes in communist countries began to have a similar impact on Mongolia. Several newly formed opposition parties organized peaceful demonstrations, demanding political and economic reforms. The most prominent of these parties was the Mongolian Democratic Union, founded in December 1989.

As new opposition groups emerged and public demonstrations increased, a crisis of confidence occurred within the ruling Mongolian People's Revolutionary Party (MPRP) and the entire communist leadership of Mongolia resigned. Jambyn Batmönh was replaced by Punsalmaagiyn Ochirbat as the head of state in 1990.

The ruling party responded to people's demands, expelling Yumjaagiyn Tsedenbal, its general secretary, and rehabilitating those purged by him in the 1960s. Foreign investments were encouraged through new laws. Previously the government had enforced collective ownership of all livestock—everything was owned by the state, and the number of animals people could personally own was limited. These limits have now been removed. The many new opposition parties that formed were legalized.

In July 1990 the first democratic general election was held. This brought into existence a parliamentary government with a president and, for the first time, representatives from more than one political party in the State Great Hural.

Still, the MPRP was strongly in control of government. Of the 430 deputies in the State Great Hural, 357 were MPRP candidates. Also elected were candidates from the Mongolian Democratic Party, the Mongolian Revolutionary Youth League, the Mongolian National Progress Party, and the Mongolian Social-Democratic Party, as well as some independent candidates.

In the years following the 1992 election, the opposition parties regrouped. Four of them formed the Mongolian National Democratic Party, and another four became the Coalition of Four Unions. A United Heritage Party emerged as well as the Mongolian Democratic Renewal Party. All pressured the government for change and an improvement in living standards. Demonstrations and hunger strikes were held in Sukhebaatar Square from 1993 to 1995.

A new constitution in 1992 made two important changes—it reduced the number of members of the State Great Hural to 76, all belonging to one house, and changed the name of the country from the Mongolian People's Republic to, simply, Mongolia. The election results that year showed that the MPRP was still popular; it won 70 of the 76 seats.

The 1996 election gave the opposition parties their first victory. The Democratic Alliance, a coalition of opposition parties, won 50 seats in the State Great Hural. The MPRP took only 25 seats, and the United Heritage Party one.

Radnaasumbereliyn Gonchigdorj, the leader of the Mongolian Social-Democratic Party (a member of the Democratic Alliance), became chairman of the State Great Hural. The leader of the Alliance, Mendsaikhanu Enkhsaikhan, became the prime minister. The president continued to be P. Ochirbat, who had replaced Batmönh in 1990 and had his position confirmed by the people in direct elections in 1993. In May 1997, however, Ochirbat's popularity waned. He lost the presidential election to Natsagiin Bagabandi, chairman of the MPRP.

New elections in May 1998 brought the Democracy Union coalition into power and its leader Tsahiagin Elbegdorj became the new prime minister.

INDEPENDENT AND SOVEREIGN

The constitution adopted in 1960 was changed in 1992 and further revised in 1996. In its present form, it has shed much of its former communist ideology and reflects the move toward democratic reform of the government and an open-market economy.

The constitution declares Mongolia to be an independent and sovereign republic. It upholds the ideals of democracy, justice, freedom, equality, national unity, and respect for the law. Total power is vested in the people and is exercised through their direct participation in state affairs and through elected representatives.

The state recognizes all forms of public and private property, including private ownership of land, but reserves the right to confiscate private land if it has been used for a purpose contrary to the national interest.

Human rights and freedoms are guaranteed, including the right to social assistance in old age, disability, childbirth, and child care. Citizens have the right to free medical aid, and free basic education.

Opposite: **A Mongolian casts his vote in the first free election in July 1990.**

THE MONGOLIAN PEOPLE'S REVOLUTIONARY PARTY

The Mongolian People's Revolutionary Party (MPRP) is Mongolia's oldest, and for a very long time, its only political party. It ruled the country from 1921 until 1996. Before the revolution of 1921, there were no political parties in Mongolia.

The MPRP was established March 1, 1921, at a meeting of 17 Mongolian revolutionaries in the border town of Hiagt (now Troitskosavsk in Russia). It is now the largest opposition party with 25 seats in the State Great Hural. The leader or chairman of the party is the country's current president, Natsagiin Bagabandi. The general secretary of the party is Nambaryn Enkhbayar. Since the move toward greater political freedom and expression in the 1990s began, the MPRP has given up its former Marxist-Leninist communist philosophy. Instead, it proclaims democratic socialist principles. The party has more than 80,000 members.

FOREIGN RELATIONS

In the 1990s, despite reforms toward democratic freedoms and a market economy, ties with the Russian Federation and the other newly independent socialist countries continued to be strong. Ties with China also improved although historically they have not been smooth. Mongolia is striving for friendly relations with the United States, Germany and the other developed Western nations, Japan, and other Asian nations.

POLITICAL LEADERS

Natsagiin Bagabandi (1950–), president of Mongolia, was elected on May 18, 1997, for a five-year term. He was born in Zavhan *aimag* in northwest Mongolia. He received his technical education from the Leningrad Technical School in the former Soviet Union. After three years as a mechanic at a vodka and beer factory in Ulaanbaatar, he continued his education in the Odessa Food Technology Institute in the Soviet Union and became a technology engineer. He ventured into politics when he was 30, joining the Mongolian People's Revolutionary Party as its propagandist, and later as a head of department of the party's central committee. In 1984 Bagabandi went to the Moscow Social Science Academy where he branched into philosophy and graduated a year later. In 1992 he was elected to the State Great Hural and was appointed chairman. He was reelected in 1996. That same year he was made first chairman of the Mongolian People's Revolutionary Party.

Tsahiagiin Elbegdorj (1963–) was born in Hovd province where he received his early education. Upon graduation from high school in Erdenet, he attended the Military Political Institute in the Soviet Union where he majored in military journalism. When he returned to Mongolia, he spent a year in the armed forces. In 1988 he joined the Military Publications Office as a correspondent, rapidly rising to become editor-in-chief. His political career began in 1989 as leader of the Democratic Union, a coalition formed by the Mongolian National Democratic Party and the Mongolian Social Democratic Party. He was elected to the State Great Hural in 1992 and in 1996 was appointed its deputy speaker. In April 1998 he became prime minister.

ROLE OF THE ARMY

The Mongolian army was at its most formidable in the 13th century at the height of the great Mongol empire. From the waning of the empire in the 16th century to the beginning of the 20th century, the influence of the Lamaist Buddhist religion resulted in almost half the male population becoming monks.

The modern Mongolian army traces its beginnings to March 1921 when the rebel forces under Sukhebaatar and Choibalsan defeated both Chinese and White Russian army forces to liberate Mongolia from foreign invaders. In 1939 Mongolian forces helped Soviet forces repel a Japanese invasion from Manchuria. Mongolia also gave support to Soviet forces during World War II.

Today the armed forces are made up of troops for general defense, air defense, construction, and civil defense. All Mongolian males reaching the age of 18 are obliged by law to do military service for a year. Those who have completed their service are placed in the reserve.

Soldiers stand at attention for the National Day Parade.

ECONOMY

MONGOLIA'S ECONOMIC DEVELOPMENT can be divided into three periods—the traditional economy before the revolution, the socialist economy after 1921, and the emerging market economy from the late 1980s to the present. The economy is now in transition toward an open-market economy. Formerly, the government set production targets for farms and factories. Today, its goal is to revive the national economy by increasing the level of private ownership and creating favorable conditions for foreign investment. Individual enterprise is encouraged. The nomadic herder is still important to the economy, and so is the urban entrepreneur.

ENTERING THE 20TH CENTURY

Traditionally, Mongolia's subsistence economy was based on nomadic animal husbandry. Most of the population were herders. Herders owned

The State Property Committee is responsible for implementing and monitoring the privatization program adopted by the government in July 1997. It decides on privatization policies and procedures.

Left: **Miners in their work gear.**

Opposite: **The State Department Store.**

THREE ECONOMIC REGIONS

In the late 1980s, Mongolia was divided into three economic regions. The central economic region is the most productive. It covers the Selenge, Bulgan, Hövsgöl, Töv, Arhangai, Övöhangai, Bayanhongor, Dundgov', Önögov', and Dornogov' *aimag*. About 70% of the population live in this region, which includes the major industrial centers of Ulaanbaatar, Darhan, and Erdenet. It has the richest mineral deposits, the best agricultural land, and the most developed network of power supply, transportation, and communications. It is responsible for about 90% of the national industrial output and more than 60% of the national agricultural output.

The eastern economic region consists of the Sukhebaatar, Dornod, and Hentii *aimag*. It occupies a quarter of the country and about a tenth of the people live there. Most of the land is steppeland, which is rich pastureland. There is some mining, mainly of tungsten, fluorspar, and brown coal. This region produces about 8% of the national industrial output and 15% of the national agricultural output.

The western economic region includes the Bayan-Ölgi, Uvs, Hovd, Zavhan, and Gov'altai *aimag*. It is a little more populated than the eastern region—more than 20% of the population live here—but it contributes only 6% of the national industrial output and about 20% of the national agricultural output. Nevertheless, the western region is believed to be economically promising, especially in its mineral resources, which remain to be developed. It produces animal husbandry products, timber and other building materials, and minerals.

livestock or tended the herds belonging to the rich and the monasteries. They produced necessities from the animals, kept what they needed, and gave the rest in rent. There was hardly any farming or industry. Trade and businesses were mostly run by the Chinese.

After the revolution the communist government began to grow crops and launch industries based on the processing of animal products. Mining, forestry, and consumer goods industries were developed as well as a railway and industrial complexes. The government controlled all trade, finance, transportation, and communications. Collectivization was introduced, livestock taken over from private owners, and state farms established. All production targets were set by the state in five-year plans.

In the late 1980s, however, the government realized that there was overcentralization and that plans were being met regardless of the costs. The government introduced democratic reforms. Since its privatization policy was implemented, more than 10,000 private businesses have begun, although the new entrepreneurs still need experience and expertise.

ANIMAL HUSBANDRY AND AGRICULTURE

A woman provides water
for her animals.

Breeding livestock is the main economic activity; its main product is meat. Since collectivization was reversed, herders are allowed to own more animals and limits on private ownership have been removed. By mid-1995, more than 90% of all livestock was privately owned.

There are more than 12 million sheep, almost 60% of all livestock. Wool is produced from sheep and camels. Cattle, horses, goats, and camels provide meat, skins, and milk. Mongolia has industrial cattle farms and mechanized dairies. Two million gallons or more (over nine million liters) of *airag* ("AI-rug"), an alcoholic drink made from mare's milk, are consumed annually.

Farming in Mongolia is very limited and difficult due to the harsh climate. The main crops are cereals, mainly wheat. Barley, oats, and millet are grown mostly as fodder. Potatoes, cabbages, carrots, turnips, onions, garlic, cucumbers, tomatoes, and lettuce are the main vegetables grown. All produce is consumed domestically.

With the change to a market economy, herders who had relied for years on collectives to sell their produce are now facing difficulty— they must learn to sell in the open market and find their own buyers.

FORESTRY AND FISHING

Mongolia's vast forests produce timber for construction and for fuel. The animals in the forests and steppes, such as marmots, squirrels, foxes, wolves, and deer, are hunted for their fur, meat, and other products. Animal hides are exported.

There is also a very small fishing industry and canned fish is exported.

MINING

Until the 1920s mining was confined to coal. The Nalaih coal mine near Ulaanbaatar is the country's oldest coal mine. Yet, Mongolia is rich not only in coal but also in copper, fluorspar, gold, iron ore, lead, tin, wolfram, and uranium. In the 1970s valuable mineral deposits of copper, molybdenum, wolfram, fluorspar, gold, and tin were discovered, but much of this has yet to be exploited. Mongolia is a leading world producer and exporter of copper, molybdenum, and fluorspar. Mining is an important sector, accounting for more than 60% of exports.

ENERGY

Most of the country's coal goes to fuel power stations. Mongolia produces 5 million tons (4.5 million metric tonnes) of coal a year, a small proportion of the country's reserve of at least 100 billion tons (91 billion metric tonnes).

Power stations are very visible in Ulaanbaatar and other towns. Most *aimag* centers have thermal power stations or diesel generators. In the rural areas people still collect wood and dry animal dung to use as fuel.

Some coal is exported to Russia by rail in exchange for electricity. In 1995 fuel and energy made up more than 18% of imports. Mongolia is exploring alternative sources of fuel; it is prospecting for oil and gas, and developing wind and solar power.

LIGHT INDUSTRY

Factories in Ulaanbaatar and Erdenet turn out carpets, knitwear, cashmere, camel wool, and felt products. Mongolia is one of the world's biggest producers of cashmere. The food industry has meat-packing plants, dairies, and flour mills and produces canned meat, sausage, butter, soap, and other commodities. There are also woodworking, paper, furniture, and construction enterprises that depend on the forestry industry.

Urban Mongolians at a bus stop.

CONSTRUCTION

The construction industry has been important in modernizing Mongolia. China provided labor, materials, and expertise to help build brick and glass works, timber works, housing estates, and other projects. By the early 1990s, Mongolia had almost 100 national construction companies.

There are brick, cement, and reinforced concrete plants, and timber mills in Ulaanbaatar, Darhan, and other towns. Housing construction continues to cater for the increase in population.

TRANSPORTATION AND COMMUNICATIONS

Carts, drawn by horse, camel, or yak, have given way to modern transport by road and rail. Construction of the first hard surface roads began in the late 1920s. In 1925 Mongolia established a state transportation committee with 12 trucks. Mongolia has about 4,350 miles (7,000 km) of roads, but only about 700 miles (1,125 km) are paved.

Much of the development of modern transportation was done with Soviet aid, especially roads and bridges. Railroad construction began in the late 1930s. The Trans-Mongolian Railway links Ulaanbaatar with Moscow in the north and Beijing in the southeast. Almost all of Mongolia's imports and exports are moved by rail.

Water transportation is not extensive as Mongolia is landlocked. It has about 250 miles (400 km) of navigable waterways, mainly on Lake Hövsgöl and the Selenge River, for carrying goods to and from Russia.

Air transportation is important because Mongolia's small population is spread over a large area. Mongolian Airlines, or MIAT, the international carrier, runs a regular air service to most of the country's cooperative and

Train carriages and other rolling stock were manufactured with Soviet aid.

THE MESSENGER SYSTEM

In the 13th century, Mongolia had a sophisticated communications system of horse relay. All herders had to contribute horses to this system. Horse relay stations, or *örtöö* ("OOR-taw"), were maintained at intervals 20–30 miles (30–50 km) apart along the main routes crossing the Mongol empire. A court messenger could arrive at any station and be assured of being fed and having a rest, as well as receiving a fresh mount for the rest of his journey.

Marco Polo wrote, "Whatever route the messenger took from the capital ... he would arrive at an *örtöö,* each of which maintained some 300 to 400 horses, always ready to take the messenger on. There are premises for accommodating and lodging the messengers, and every other thing they might require."

The *örtöö* system was like the Pony Express that linked North America from coast to coast from 1860 to 1861, although the Pony Express was mainly a mail service with stations 25–75 miles (40–120 km) apart. Unlike the Pony Express riders, who handed their saddlebags to another rider at the next relay station, the Mongolian couriers rode the full distance themselves, often covering 50–70 miles (80–110 km) a day, stopping only briefly if at all for some food and rest. They would strap themselves up tightly with leather belts to keep from falling off their horses.

The *örtöö* system helped to build and administer the Mongol empire by providing quick and efficient communication between the khan and his far-ranging army. It remained functioning until the early 20th century. In 1913 there were still 150 stations on the main roads that passed through the capital and crossed the country from north to south and from east to west.

state farms as well as provides crop-dusting services, forest and steppe air patrols, and air ambulance services—on top of carrying passengers, freight, and mail. There are 81 airports in Mongolia, including its one international airport near Ulaanbaatar. Mongolia has air links with Moscow, Beijing, and Berlin.

In 1921 the revolutionary government nationalized postal and telecommunication services that had been Russian-, Chinese-, and Danish-owned, and established a postal and telegraph department. Soviet aid helped Mongolia develop its communication networks.

In Ulaanbaatar it is possible to make international phone calls, and to send and receive faxes. Where satellite television is available, one can receive international news. There is also an Internet and e-mail service provider in the city.

BANKING AND FINANCIAL SERVICES

Until 1924 Mongolia did not have its own banks or a currency. There was barter trade, using livestock, tea, and salt. Within the country, Russian and Chinese currencies were used, while foreign trade was in US dollars and the British pound. Most of the banks that existed at the time were owned by the Chinese.

The revolutionary government reformed the system and established the Mongolbank in 1924. It is now known as the Trade and Development Bank of Mongolia. A year later the government introduced the *tögrög* ("TOOG-roog") as the national currency. All debts to moneylenders and foreign merchants were canceled, and private lending was outlawed. All state enterprises had to keep their money with the state bank, which controlled all the financial transactions in the country.

Above: **A new bank under construction.**

Left. **Traditional living does not mean living without modern conveniences such as a motorcycle and satellite dish.**

FOREIGN TRADE

Before the 1990s Mongolia's main trading partners were the Soviet Union and the East European countries. Trade with other communist countries increased after Mongolia joined the Council for Mutual Economic Assistance (COMECON) in 1962.

Until the 1980s Mongolia continued to import more than it exported; the Soviet Union was its major trading partner. In 1996 Mongolia imported most of its goods from the Russian Federation, Japan, and China. The main imports are machinery, mineral products, and transport equipment. The main export markets are Switzerland, the Russian Federation, China, Japan, and Korea. Mongolia exports mainly mineral products and textiles.

Production workers in a food factory.

Many Mongolians dislike the rigid discipline and schedule of the urban workplace. They are used to a lifestyle of freedom of movement and work that follows the seasons.

WORKERS

With economic development, the labor force has grown dramatically. From 1960 to 1983 the number of workers doubled, and today almost half of them are engaged in material production. Most workers have had eight to nine years of school. Mongolians generally worked an eight-hour day and enjoyed 15 days paid vacation a year.

Industrial and office workers and their families form about 70% of the population. Two-fifths of the working population are in agriculture, and a quarter in industry, transportation, administration, and services.

In the cities the closure of state enterprises has worsened the problem of unemployment. According to United Nations official statistics, more than 57,000 people are unemployed. The number of poor in the country is 446,000, comprising more than 19% of the population.

TOURISM INDUSTRY

The tourism industry is growing in importance. There used to be just one government-run tourist agency, Juulchin; it has been privatized but remains the biggest agency in Mongolia. Now there are as many as 100 travel agencies. Ulaanbaatar has several hotels, from cheap dormitory-style accommodation to the fancy Ulaan Baatar, Bayangol, and Chinggis Khaan hotels.

The mountains attract climbers, and tourists come to enjoy other outdoor activities including skiing and ice-skating, camping, hiking, fishing, riding, and kayaking. There are even tourist *ger* so the visitor can get a taste of living Mongolian style.

The three main tourist centers are Terelj, northeast of Ulaanbaatar, Hujirt in the southwest, and the Gobi Desert center.

Tourists pose with an extended Mongolian family in a *ger*.

THE MONGOLIAN STOCK EXCHANGE

The Mongolian Stock Exchange (MSE) was created in 1991 as part of the country's program to privatize state-owned companies and develop a capital market. From 1992 to 1995 there was free distribution of vouchers to all Mongolian citizens for buying shares in companies on the exchange. Then, starting in August 1995, the MSE began functioning as a regular stock exchange, with a listing of 470 companies. The Mongolian Securities Commission, created in 1995, is charged with regulating and controlling activities in the securities market.

TOWARD A MARKET ECONOMY

The change to a market economy caused an economic crisis in the early 1990s with the collapse of trade and foreign aid ties with the former Soviet

Union. Industrial production dropped because of fuel shortages and distribution problems, and basic foodstuffs had to be rationed. Inflation was 325% in 1992. After the opposition came to power in 1996, wide-ranging economic reforms were implemented. Government spending has been cut, insolvent banks closed, utility prices raised, and foreign investment welcomed. Inflation dropped to 35%, and a four-year economic program was announced that allows more private ownership of state property.

The government is concentrating on further reducing inflation and increasing the country's gross domestic product. In April 1997 the State Great Hural voted to abolish all duties and trade taxes.

Mongolia joined the Group of 77 in 1989; in 1991 the International Monetary Fund, World Bank, and Asian Development Bank; and in 1997, the World Trade Organization.

MONGOLIANS

MONGOLIA IS ONE OF THE most sparsely populated countries in the world and has an uneven population distribution. The most densely populated regions are the river valleys of forested mountain slopes and the grasslands; the least populated areas are the desert, semidesert, and mountainous regions. Mongolians are a largely unknown people, because during most of its history, the country was closed to the Western world. The exception was during the 13th century, when the Mongol empire was at its strongest. What was known about the Mongols was mixed with fable and fear. Mongolia is now more open and accessible.

ETHNIC GROUPS

There are two main ethnic groups—the Mongolian group and the Turkic group. The majority of the people fall into the Mongolian group.

The medical term "mongolism" or "mongoloid" was once used to describe people with Down Syndrome. Such people were thought to resemble Mongolians. This term is now inappropriate and offensive to both Mongolians and Down Syndrome sufferers.

Left: **The *del* is worn by all age groups.**

Opposite: **A Kazakh woman getting ready to prepare a meal.**

A Kazakh family at prayer before the ritual slaughter of sheep.

Of this group, 70% are the nomadic Khalkha Mongols who live mainly in the eastern and central part of the country. The word *khalkha* ("HAL-ha") means shield and originated around the 17th century when the Mongols of the east decided to form an alliance or shield in their struggle against the Manchu or Qing dynasty of China.

The other people in this group are the Döröd, Buriat, Barga, Üzemchin, Darhad, Zahchin, Bayad, Myangat, Dariganga, Ööld, Torguut, Harchin, Tsahar, and Hotgon people. These Mongols live mainly in the west and northwest and along the southeast border with China.

There are small differences among these groups and their dialects so they understand each other. Their ethnic clothes also vary little from group to group, perhaps only in the kind of headdress worn or in the shape of the shoes.

The second ethnic group are the Turkic people, the Kazakhs, who make up 6% of the population. They are a pastoral people living mainly in the extreme western part of the country, in the Altai region, and are traditionally Muslims. They are well-known hunters who hunt on horseback and use trained golden eagles and greyhounds to attack prey. Many Kazakhs work in the coal mines of north-central Mongolia. Tuvinians, Urianhai, and Uighurs are all Turkic peoples.

A small number of Russians and Chinese live permanently in Mongolia. In the early 1920s, many Chinese in Mongolia were merchants, traders, and artisans who worked in the Buddhist monasteries. Many Russians came to Mongolia as advisors and skilled workers during the communist period, married Mongol women, and became assimilated into the local population.

It is estimated that by the year 2000 the population of Mongolia will have reached 2.8 million.

POPULATION CHANGES

Mongolia is a fast-growing society. Since the early 1920s, an improvement in healthcare and living standards has made it possible for the population to increase quite rapidly. Just before the revolution, there were only about half a million people. Today, the population has more than tripled, increasing at about twice the growth rate for the rest of the world. This very rapid growth rate of 2.6% (1992) means that Mongolia has a very young society. In 1989 children 15 years old and younger made up 42% of the population. People under 35 accounted for three-quarters of the population.

As the country continues to modernize and industrialize, the migration of people from rural areas to the cities is also expected to grow. In 1989 the proportion of rural to urban inhabitants was 48% to 52% respectively.

Almost half of all Mongolian families consist of five or more people. Better healthcare has also increased the life expectancy of the average Mongolian man to 63 years and of the average woman to 68 years. There used to be more men than women, but today there is an almost equal proportion of men and women in the population.

Above: **A Buddhist lama in his red robe.**

Opposite: **Children in a nursery.**

A FEUDAL SOCIETY

Before the 1921 revolution, Mongolian society was a feudal society with no social mobility. At the top were the feudal lords claiming descent from Chinggis Khan. The commoners worked for the feudal lords by herding their livestock and doing military duty when requested.

There was very little formal education and it was difficult to change one's status in society. The only form of "escape" was through the Buddhist monasteries. Young boys and men could offer their service to the monasteries where they could be educated and make monastic service their career.

The lamas were also a politically and socially powerful class of people in this feudal Mongolian society, but their influence was destroyed when the communists came to power in the 1920s.

Most of the population, about 90%, were common serfs and low-level monks. The aristocrats, who formed about 8% of the population, were the political leaders and administrators.

SOCIETY IS REVOLUTIONIZED

The structure of Mongolian society underwent a major change after the revolution, as feudalism was seen as counter to communism.

Power and wealth was taken away from the feudal lords and the powerful monasteries and redistributed among the people. Mongolian herders, who used to be self-sufficient, were formed into herding collectives or attached to state factories and mines. A monetary system was introduced, and people earned wages for their work. They were supervised by a new class of managers and administrators belonging to the Mongolian People's Revolutionary Party.

There was much emphasis on planning, projects, and meeting goals and targets. Everything was done for the collective good of society. Workers and their units competed to do a job quickly or surpass a production quota. They received benefits such as free medical care and education, and pensions when they retired. Those who excelled at their job were honored as "number one" workers. Most people were party members.

A formal education became important, and most young Mongolians were enrolled in schools where they also learned the new party ideology. They were taught punctuality, rules and standards, and the need to meet goals.

The bureaucrats and high-ranking party members were the elite. These people have post-secondary education. Next came the professionals, technicians, engineers, doctors, and others. Then there were the administrators and workers in the factories and state farms.

On the fringes were the traditional herders whose income depended on the weather, health of the herds, and the performance of their herding collective.

COLORFUL ROBES

The traditional dress for both Mongolian men and women is a long, flowing robe tied at the waist by a sash. It looks much like a dressing gown that is fastened from the throat and down the right shoulder by small cloth buttons. It has a small stand-up collar. This gown is called the *del.*

Beneath the *del,* Mongolians wear heavy trousers that are tucked into knee-high boots made of leather or felt with pointed toes. These boots are several sizes too large so that as the weather gets colder, thick socks of wool or fur can be used to pad the boots and keep the wearer warm and comfortable. Russian army boots are also very popular.

Above: **Mongolian girls bundled up against the cold with thick scarves.**

Opposite: **A Mongolian hunter in his fur cap and coat, on his motorcycle.**

FAMOUS MONGOLIANS

Dashdorjin Natsagdorj (1906–37) is considered the father of contemporary Mongolian literature. Most Mongolians know by heart his famous poem, *My Motherland,* glorifying Mongolia as an old country renewed and with a promising future. *The Four Seasons of the Year* is about Mongolia and building a new Mongolia. The poem *Star* explores the possibility of flights into space. Natsagdorj was also a playwright and author of *Three Tragic Fates,* the first Mongolian opera.

Balduugiyn Sharav (1869–1939), a celebrated painter, spent his childhood in a monastery and later traveled all over Mongolia. The common subject of his paintings was the simple life and traditions of the people. He used traditional techniques. *One Day in the Life of Mongolia,* his masterpiece, is full of intricate drawings covering many aspects of Mongolian life.

Both the *del*, which reaches down to below the knees, and the sash are often very colorful. The *del* is commonly worn in the rural areas. In the winter it has an inner lining of sheepskin or red fox fur that keeps the wearer warm. The color and shape of the *del* are differentiated according to the different ethnic groups.

In the summer men sometimes wear a Western-style felt hat or Russian-style cap; in the winter, a warmer fur cap with earflaps to keep the ears warm.

City people, especially office workers, are more often found in Western-style clothes. The women wear dresses and the men dull-colored shirts, suits, and shoes. But almost everybody has a festive or special *del* reserved for more formal occasions.

Young people are like their contemporaries in other cities in the world. They love wearing jeans, shirts, and jackets; the girls wear dresses.

The hair of the women is long and often plaited or coiled at the back of the head.

When a Mongol woman gets married, she is dressed in traditional finery that usually includes an extremely elaborate headdress and heavy jewelry made from silver and semi-precious stones. The style of the headdress varies from one ethnic group to another.

LIFESTYLE

THE PRACTICE OF PASTORALISM is still important in Mongolian life. It shapes the way Mongolians generally see the world. They value the freedom of movement that is characteristic of a nomadic life. They love the countryside and have a close affinity with nature, which has such a major effect on their daily lives, and with their animals, with which they have an interdependent or symbiotic relationship. Even young Mongolians living in the cities will go out to the country whenever they can.

THE MODERN NOMAD

Traditional herding has been modernized. Horses are still important but are supplemented with jeeps, trucks, and motorcycles. Herders can get the latest weather reports and storm warnings on transistor radios. At winter camps, portable power generators provide energy.

Mongolians have a saying: "Erhuni jargal, idsugui heer," *meaning,* "Man's joy is in wide-open and empty spaces."

Left: **Motorcycles can fill up at pumps in the countryside.**

Opposite. **A young girl and her ewes.**

A group of herders having a celebration at their camp site.

Herding collectives often have the same boundaries as the district's administrative center. The centers provide services to the herders and their families—a school, storage facilities, cinemas, health facilities, a repair station, and offices. The average household owns a television set, radio, sewing machine, and a bicycle, motorcycle, or truck.

The herding camp has two to six households, sometimes related families, managing the livestock together. A family can be part of one camp one year, and move on to another the next. Some families remain with one camp for a long time. Herders do not own any grazing ground, but there is an understanding that each camp has the right to use certain areas.

During the summer months, the herds are moved over a vast area to places with good grazing ground and abundant water. In the wintertime, the camp moves to a site where there is water, dried grass, and shelter from storms. Those animals not expected to survive the harsh winter are killed in the late fall to reduce the herd size. The meat is dried and stored for the winter when neither sheep nor horses produce milk.

FIVE IMPORTANT ANIMALS

Mongolians have always depended for their well-being on five animals—the horse, camel, sheep, cattle or yak, and goat. These are known as "the five snouts or muzzles of livestock" and appear in every aspect of Mongol life, art, and literature. Not every herder has all five, but many have more than one type. The horse is the most important. It is seldom used as a draft animal, but is ridden. It also provides products like *airag,* horsehair rope, and horsehide leather. Apart from the meat, milk, and other dairy produce, dried dung of the animals is useful as fuel. Leather products are made from the hides. In the mountains especially, the yak is useful. Camels are beasts of burden in the desert for transport. Sheep's and goat's wool are used for winter clothing and to make the felt that is used to cover the *ger.* The men look after the horses, while the women tend the other animals.

Dogs are important to the Mongolian herders who often have fierce watchdogs to guard the family home. At night they protect the flocks from wolves and other predators. When someone approaches a ger, *he often calls out from far away so that the owner can come out and restrain his dog.*

A young herder checking his sheep in the pen.

THE GER

Mongolians traditionally live in a dome-shaped structure called a *ger*. Its portability makes it ideal for a nomadic lifestyle. Although apartment buildings are found in cities, most Mongolians in the country and small towns still live in *ger*. Even in Ulaanbaatar, the capital, clusters of *ger* dot the outskirts. A city *ger* often has electricity, while one in the country depends on candles and lamps for lighting.

A large brick or metal stove for heat and cooking sits in the middle, its stovepipe rising through a roof-vent. At the sides of the *ger* there may be some low, steel-framed beds curtained off. There are large decorated

A Mongolian sits in his beautifully furnished *ger*.

ERECTING A GER

The floor of the *ger* is first assembled. Next, the lattice walls are joined end to end to form the lower, circular part of the *ger*, and the door, which always faces south, is erected. The walls are made of thin wooden strips fastened in a crisscross lattice enabling the wall to be opened and shut like a concertina. The size of the *ger* depends on the number of lattice walls; there may be up to 12 walls in a large *ger*.

When the circular wall is finished, the two wooden posts are set up in the middle of the floor. The small wooden wheel forming the opening in the roof is carefully balanced on them. Long roof poles, painted orange like the sun, are inserted into slots on the wheel so that they radiate from the center like the ribs of a big umbrella. Then the lower ends of the poles are attached to the lattice walls with leather loops. A layer of canvas is stretched tightly over the roof. Thickly padded felt curtains are hung from the walls for insulation. Then, layer upon layer of felt is spread on the roof. In the winter, more felt layers are put on. Finally, the whole structure is covered with white canvas to keep out the rain. The hole at the top is covered by a small triangle of canvas, adjusted by cords from the ground. It can be opened to let in light and air and allow smoke to leave, or closed in bad weather. A second, smaller *ger* may be erected for extra storage space.

The average weight of a *ger* without furniture is about 550 pounds (250 kg). It takes about an hour and a half to erect it. When the family moves, the *ger* is taken down and placed on a cart pulled by yaks, camels, or horses.

storage chests for clothing and other items, a few mirrors, and photographs and religious pictures on the walls. A low table and some small metal folding chairs occupy the center. The wooden floor is covered with rugs. The man's working tools, his saddle, and the leather bag containing *airag* are on the man's side on the left, under the sky god's protection; the kitchen and cooking utensils are on the woman's side on the right, under the sun's protection. The back of the *ger* is reserved for elders, honored guests, and the family altar. The posts symbolize the link with heaven; it is bad manners to lean against them. A little bag holding herbs to ward off evil spirits is hung from the top. Mongolians never stand or step on the threshold of the door but step over it.

A legend regarding the ger *says that the first Mongol was born when a fair-haired man came through the opening at the top and impregnated Alangua, the mother of the Mongols.*

65

In the nomadic society of the Mongolians, the community is based on helping one another. It is said that the ger *door is seldom locked even though the owner is out herding the animals, and any tired traveler can enter and warm himself by the fire, have a rest, and take some food. For the nomads, a visitor is also very welcome as the days on the steppes can be long and lonely.*

MAKING FELT

Felt is important; it is used to cover the *ger,* and make rugs, saddle pads, and the linings of boots. Felt is made in the fall, and practically everyone takes part in the making. It is usually made from sheep's wool as wool fibers have minute barb-like scales that interlock when they are processed.

The wool is first beaten to loosen the fibers and mix them up. An old piece of felt is placed on the ground and wet. Then three layers of wool are carefully spread on top of this and the wool is drenched with water. A layer of grass is sprinkled on top.

Next, the four layers (the old felt with the three layers of new wool) are tightly rolled up—the grass sprinkled on top prevents the new wool from sticking together. The roll is thoroughly wet again, then wrapped in leather and tied with leather thongs. Two riders on horses pull the roll back and forth until the fibers of the new wool interlock and are tightly compressed to form new felt.

When the roll is unfurled, the new felt is watered down and then allowed to dry. This wetting and drying process shrinks the felt, making it dense and durable.

ROLE OF WOMEN

Women are about half the population. In the traditional nomadic society still found in rural areas, women help to milk, feed, and look after the animals when they have young. They cook and prepare the meat and dairy products, and grind the grain. Their important contribution to the functioning of the household gives them status, and they have a say in family matters. Before the revolution, women could not choose their husbands nor could they divorce them; they were completely dependent.

After the revolution women became educated. They could work outside their homes and earn a living, and they could vote. Pregnant women received special benefits at work, in line with the policy to encourage larger families. Mongolian women found work as teachers, nurses, doctors, technicians, factory workers, and businesswomen.

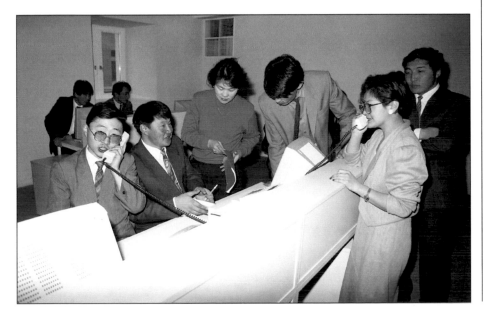

More than 20 women's organizations promote the women's movement, legal issues, equal opportunities for work, and better healthcare. The Mongolian Women's Federation, the oldest women's organization in the country, has more than 30 member organizations. The Mongolian Business Women's Federation was established in 1992.

Male and female stockbrokers at the stock exchange.

Above: **The Palace of Weddings in Ulaanbaatar.**

Opposite: **An extended Mongol family.**

The modern Mongol family is usually a nuclear one, with parents, children, and sometimes a grandparent.

The constitution guarantees equal rights with men. Abortion was legalized in 1989.

With the changeover to a market economy in the 1990s, women were the more badly affected. When state-run factories closed and government departments cut wages and reduced their staff, more women than men lost jobs and income. The social support and healthcare systems that had allowed women to work were curtailed, childcare facilities became expensive or closed, and maternity benefits were reduced.

GETTING MARRIED IN MONGOLIA

The process of getting married used to be a long, drawn-out affair with matchmakers and dowries that took from one to three years. An offer was first made by the groom's parents, through a matchmaker.

After the bride's parents gave a positive reply, both families would visit a lama to set a propitious date. Ten days later the groom's father and the matchmaker would call with an offering of ceremonial blue silk cloth. Six months after the date was set, the groom visited and there would be a small party. Six months after that gifts were exchanged. On the wedding day the groom would take the bride away to her new home, a new *ger* built by the groom near the bride's *ger*. Her first duty was to make tea for the guests; then the festivities began.

Most modern Mongolians choose their own partner and marry at the Wedding Palace, or state marriage registry, and later celebrate with a feast. Divorces are few, but said to be increasing.

Up to the 19th century Mongols traced descent through the male line. Mongols now use just a single given name; from this name, ancestors cannot be traced.

HEALTHCARE

Mongolians used to rely on traditional Mongolian and Tibetan medicine and treatments based on local folk beliefs. Modern medical services are provided by clinics and hospitals, and teaching preventive healthcare to the people was one of the priorities of the revolutionary government. Infectious diseases such as smallpox, plague, poliomyelitis, and diphtheria were a major problem caused by poor health habits, such as infrequent baths, and the difficulty of getting clean drinking water. Great effort has been put into health education, teaching people better hygiene, and how to look after their babies and the elderly. Today, the average Mongolian

Opposite: **A traditional herbalist with his medicinal herbs.**

Below: **Women pumping water in the desert. Poor sanitation and sharing water with animals often causes many diseases.**

has a life expectancy of 65, and infant mortality has dropped to 45 per 1,000 live births. Since the democratic government cut social spending, however, health standards have reportedly fallen.

While modern medicine has found its place in Mongolia, traditional medicine has been retained. The Institute of Traditional Medicine in Ulaanbaatar does extensive research on folk medicine beliefs. It studies the ancient prescriptions and traditional methods of treatment. Special formulas use local medicinal herbs and animal parts, such as antelope horns and reindeer antlers. A wolf's intestines are supposed to be good for indigestion, and a woodchuck's gallbladder is believed to cure toothache and stomach complaints. Many animals are thus hunted for their meat and also for their body parts, although there are laws restricting the hunting of rare animals such as the Gobi bear, snow leopard, wild ass, and red wolf.

Over 400 kinds of plants have been found to have medicinal uses. The Institute has an outpatient center for acupuncture, massage, mineral water baths, and mud baths.

Marmots are very useful for medicinal purposes. Marmot oil is good for burns. For a problem with the left kidney, part of the left kidney of the marmot is eaten raw.

HIGH LITERACY RATE

In pre-revolution days, religion and education were interlinked. There was no secular education. Monasteries took on the task of teaching children Tibetan, and how to chant and pray. The older and more privileged children who proved themselves up to the task were taught subjects such as philosophy, art, astrology, and medicine in higher classes in the monasteries. But the majority, the children of herders, received no formal education at all.

Following the revolution, the government sought to eradicate illiteracy among children and adults. The first primary (elementary) school was set up just a month after the government came to power. Primary schools were quickly built. Boarding schools allowed the children of nomadic families to live comfortably away from home during the school term. The government also started a drive to educate adults. Teachers were sent to homes to teach short-term courses in the evenings. Everyone who could read and write was given the responsibility to teach those who could not do so. The international agency, UNESCO, has awarded the N.K. Krupskaya Medal to the Mongolian Institute of Language and Literature of the Academy of Sciences to

acknowledge the literacy program's success. It is estimated that more than 90% of Mongolians are now literate.

Education is free and compulsory for all children from 6 to 16. Children from the age of 3 may attend kindergarten and learn the basics of reading, writing, and counting. From 6 to 18 years, students attend vocational and technical schools, learning skills in areas such as construction, industry, transport, communication, and agriculture that allow them to later join the work force.

In 1922 the first secondary special school was set up to train teachers. There are now 18 such schools training in more than 100 fields, including education, law, and medicine.

Mongolia's State University was opened in 1942. Some departments have become separate institutions such as the Agricultural Institute, Medical Institute, and Russian Language Pedagogical Institute. The nine universities, 18 special secondary schools, and 32 vocational and technical schools have a total enrollment of about 35,000 students. There are also a number of private schools and colleges.

Above: **A nursery teacher telling her attentive class a story.**

Opposite: **A group of schoolchildren waiting for their parents to take them home.**

Promising young Mongolians used to be sent by the state to the Soviet Union for further education. Many still continue advanced studies abroad, especially in Russia and Germany.

RELIGION

ABOUT 95% OF MONGOLIANS are Buddhists. There are also Muslims and Christians. The traditional and most ancient religion in the country is shamanism, based on the belief that the spirit world is present in nature. It still survives in Mongolia, though it is not as powerful as it once was. Mongolians are by law free to follow any religion they wish. The constitution guarantees freedom of worship, a legacy handed down from Chinggis Khan's time, when the ancient capital of Karakorum was a place where many religions, including shamanism, Christianity, Islam, Confucianism, Taoism, and Buddhism, were practiced.

BUDDHISM

Buddhism came to Mongolia very early from the Uighur people, one of the most advanced civilizations in Central Asia.

The link between Mongolia and Tibet is very strong. Every Mongolian Buddhist hopes to make a pilgrimage to the holy city of Lhasa, Tibet, at least once in his lifetime.

Left: **Young lamas in Sukhebaatar Square in their colorful yellow hats and red robes.**

Opposite: **Lamas blowing conches high up on a tower in a monastery in Karakorum.**

The richly decorated entrance to a Buddhist temple.

Mongolians, like Tibetans, gain merit by turning prayer wheels, hollow cylinders filled with thousands of small paper prayer slips. Each revolution adds to the merit.

Although shamanism was the most influential religion at this time, the aristocracy including Chinggis himself was sympathetic to Buddhism. But it was only in the 13th century that Buddhism gained real influence with Kublai Khan becoming the first Mongol ruler to make Buddhism the state religion. He appointed Phagspa Lama, a Tibetan monk, as the spiritual head of the country and granted special status to all Buddhist priests, called lamas. They were exempted from military duty and taxes. However, Buddhism was not widespread as it was the religion of the ruling classes. With the collapse of Kublai's Yuan dynasty, Buddhism lost its influence in Mongolia.

Not until the 16th century did Buddhism become more widespread. Mongol society was in a bad state; many Mongol leaders were fighting for power among themselves, and people were unhappy and in despair. The rulers felt that a strong religion like Buddhism would give their position and the people moral strength. At this time, there was rivalry between the Red Hat and Yellow Hat sects of Tibetan Buddhism; each hoped to gain power through the support of the Mongols. The Chinese Ming dynasty was also anxious to have the Mongols embrace religion, hoping that Buddhism would pacify the warlike Mongols.

In 1578 the Mongol ruler Altan Khan invited the Tibetan religious head, Sonam Gyatsho, to Mongolia and gave him the title of Dalai Lama. In return, he received recognition as the reincarnation of Kublai Khan, reestablishing the spiritual links between Mongolia and Tibet. Shamanism and all its practices were effectively banned. The lamas quickly adapted shamanist rituals to Buddhist rites to help the spread of Buddhism.

From then on, Buddhism grew in influence. Translations of large numbers of Buddhist sacred texts from Tibetan into Mongolian helped to make Buddhism accessible to the people. Monasteries were built all over the country and gained in popularity and influence, mainly because the chief priests were often local princes and people with great influence in society. Many lamas were philosophers, scientists, historians, artists, and crafts people, and the monasteries became centers of learning.

Gombordorji Zanabazar, the Jebtsundamba, was a famous reincarnate lama and head of Buddhism in Mongolia. He built the Ih Hüree monastery in Urga in 1651 and many others, and translated many Buddhist texts. He was also a consummate sculptor and painter of religious statues and scrolls. Seven other Jebtsundamba rulers followed him but all were from Tibet because the Chinese Qing emperors were afraid a Mongol would cause political trouble. The eighth Jebtsundamba did, declaring Mongolia independent of Chinese rule. When he died in 1924, the communist government stopped a successor from being found.

Serene Buddha images in a temple museum in Karakorum.

Reincarnation is a basic Buddhist belief. Reincarnate lamas are found by interpreting omens and dreams, and they are tested. Zanabazar was said to be able to recite Tibetan texts at 5, without ever having learned this language.

Religious persecution began in 1932. In 1937, under Choibalsan, more than 17,000 monks vanished. Of more than 700 monasteries, only four were left standing to serve as museums of the "feudal period." Religious ceremonies were illegal except at Gandantegchinlin monastery (also called Gandan) in Ulaanbaatar until 1990. Religious practices were allowed once again in the 1990s.

MONASTERIES

In the early 1990s, the decline of communist rule led to the rehabilitation of religion. About 2,000 lamas established small communities at the sites of about 120 former monasteries, and many monasteries damaged during the persecution of the 1930s were restored.

The three big monasteries in Mongolia are the Gandan monastery in Ulaanbaatar, the Erdene Zuu in Karakorum, and the Amarbayasgalant monastery near Darhan. The Gandan, the largest and most important center of Buddhism, was built in 1838. Its library holds thousands of rare books and manuscripts in Tibetan, Mongolian, and other languages. The monastery is the headquarters of the Asian Buddhist Conference for Peace, an organization made up of members from many Asian countries.

SHAMANISM

Shamanism was very important in the spiritual life of the people until the 16th century. During the rule of Chinggis Khan, it played a big role. The people believed that Chinggis received his authority to rule from *Tengri*, the sky god. There were many shamans in Chinggis' court who acted as intermediaries between the people and the spirit world. A chief shaman determined, with the help of his bond to the spirit world, when it was time to break camp, where the khan's camp should go, if it was the right time to go to war, and many other big and small decisions.

Mongolia shares a tradition of shamanism with many other hunting-gathering cultures in Central Asia and North America. A shaman usually comes from a family with a history of shamanism. Both men and women can be shamans.

Above: **Amulets, blue ribbons, and offerings on the "hundred trunk tree," a shamanist shrine.**

Opposite: **The Erdene Zuu monastery in Karakorum, the oldest and largest in Mongolia. It once had 10,000 lamas.**

A person destined to become a shaman is usually identified by some strange behavior such as fainting spells or visions. He or she takes years to learn to communicate with the spirits. The process includes prolonged fasts, living like a hermit, and interpreting dreams and visions. The shaman helps to cure illnesses, drive away evil spirits, find lost animals, make predictions, and is consulted for a favorable date on which to hold an important event, for example, cutting a child's hair for the first time, breaking camp, or doing business.

FOLK BELIEFS

Many myths and beliefs connected with shamanism explain the relationship between the heavens and the people, the creation of the world, and the role of nature. There are three worlds—the heavenly upper world ruled by *Tengri*, the earthly middle world inhabited by people, and the subterranean lower world, lorded over by *Erleg Khan* ("ER-leg khan"). The sky is male and the earth is female.

Many folk beliefs are connected with the countryside, a belief in the sacredness of the mountains and lakes, and other natural objects. Mongolians are superstitious, believing in charms, strange events, and miracles. Everyday

OVOO

An *ovoo* ("AW-waw") is a shrine in the countryside, on a mountain slope, or near a lake or river, that often looks like a pile of stones or rocks placed in a pyramid shape. Bottles of vodka, a bit of tobacco, some colored scraps of cloth, even some money, or sweets are often placed on the *ovoo* as an offering to the gods. When a person comes across an *ovoo*, he usually walks around it three times in a clockwise direction and adds some kind of offering to the collection already there.

Every so often a small religious ceremony is held at the site of an *ovoo*. Lamas say prayers accompanied by libations or the pouring of liquor, usually *airag*, on the shrine, and people make offerings. There is usually some feasting followed by a mini-festival of sports. This ritual usually celebrates the coming of spring. It is also held to pray for good weather, abundant rainfall, plentiful grass for the animals, and successful hunting.

This ceremony, which was once prohibited, has made a reappearance with the greater freedom of democracy in the 1990s.

objects may possess magical qualities—for example, the stirrup is important and when a man leaves on a long trip, milk is sprinkled on it to bless it. Many superstitions concern animals. The peacock, for example, is sacred so Mongolian homes often have peacock feathers to purify the home. Crows and snakes are believed to cast spells, and a goose can break a man's stirrup if he does something bad to the goose. It is believed that one's very own star shines when one is born and disappears from the sky when one dies. If one is very lucky or has a happy life, it is due to one's lucky star.

Opposite: **Fire is sacred. It is never stamped out or put out with water or by smothering with dirt, but put out by carefully removing the stones used, thus releasing the fire.**

ISLAM AND CHRISTIANITY

Muslims are about 5% of the total population. Most are Kazakhs living in Bayan-Ölgi in the west. The Muslims also suffered during the persecution of religion under the communists, and many mosques were closed or destroyed. Some have been reopened or are being rebuilt.

There are very few Christians. A law passed in 1993 on state and church relations restricts religious activities to Buddhism, shamanism, and Islam. The state banned Christian involvement in government, any new missionary activity not approved by the state, and any teaching of Christianity outside churches and monasteries. Mongolian Christians have challenged this as unconstitutional.

LANGUAGE

THE MONGOLIAN LANGUAGE, like its culture, has been shaped by the many historical influences that have affected the country and its people over the centuries. This is especially so in the written form of the language.

SPOKEN LANGUAGE

Mongolian is spoken by most of the people of Mongolia and also by those living in Inner Mongolia, which is part of China. It is also spoken by other groups of people living in other provinces of China and the Russian Federation.

Mongolian is part of the Altaic family of languages that is spoken over a wide area from Turkey in the west to the Pacific Ocean in the east. Many different dialects are spoken by the various Mongol tribes but there are basically four main dialects.

Left: **Schoolchildren taking notes in class.**

Opposite: **A newspaper vendor.**

83

An example of classical Mongolian script. The earliest Mongolian writing, the Stone of Chinggis, is a 13th century inscription of the archery feats of Yisüngge, Chinggis' nephew. This stele is in the Hermitage Museum in St. Petersburg, Russia.

Khalkha, the main dialect spoken by most Mongolians, is the dialect on which the official language is based. The other three main dialects are the Western or Oirat dialects, spoken in the western parts of the country; the Buriad dialect, spoken in the north around Lake Baikal; and the Inner Mongolian dialects of the south.

Many Mongolians, having been educated in Russia, are also fluent in Russian. English is becoming a popular second language.

WRITING IT DOWN

The Mongols developed their written script using scripts borrowed from other people when a script became necessary for administrative and religious missionary work. Their script has changed many times.

The written language in use today dates back to the 13th century. According to Mongol history, Chinggis Khan decided that there should be a proper written Mongolian language. After conquering the Uighur people, he commanded his captive Uighur advisor, Tatatungo, to adapt the ancient Uighur script to the Mongolian language. The long, string-like letters were connected by continuous lines from top to bottom and read from left to right.

For a short period of time, when Kublai Khan was in power, he wanted a new written language to unite the many different languages of his empire. He ordered the Tibetan scholar and monk, Phagspa Lama, to devise a new alphabet. The Square Script, with square-shaped letters, emerged. It was based on the Tibetan and Indian alphabet and was written

THE *SOYOMBO* SCRIPT AND SYMBOL

The *Soyombo* ("SOH-yom-bo") script was introduced by Gombordorji Zanabazar in 1686. It was such a complex and ornamental script that it became impractical for wide use. Instead, it was limited to religious uses, in prayers and religious texts. What has remained of this script, however, is the *Soyombo* symbol, which has been adopted as the Mongolian national emblem of freedom and independence. It is depicted in the state emblem and in the national flag.

At the very top is a five-pointed star. Below is a flame symbolizing blossoming, revival, and the continuation of the family. The three points of the flame symbolize the past, present, and future prosperity of the people. Below the flame is the sun and the crescent moon, symbolizing the origin of the Mongolian people. The flame, sun, and moon together express the wish that the Mongolian people may always live and prosper.

Next come some geometric forms—triangles and rectangles. The triangles express the wish for freedom and independence, while the horizontal rectangles at the sides symbolize honesty, justice, and nobility. The broader, vertical rectangles symbolize the walls of a fortress. In the middle of the geometric section of the emblem are two intertwined fish, like the Chinese *yin yang* symbol, symbolizing the unity of men and women. In Mongolian folklore, fish never close their eyes and are therefore vigilant creatures. This part of the *Soyombo* expresses the wish that people will be united so that they will be stronger than the walls of a fortress.

from top to bottom. It was the official script of the Yuan dynasty. When Kublai's rule ended, the script fell into disuse. Examples of this script remain in inscriptions in temples, seals, and title pages of ancient books.

In the 17th century, two other scripts were invented. Both the Clear Script, which tried to bring the written language closer to the spoken language, and the Horizontal Square Script based on an ancient form of Indian writing could transcribe and record words in Mongolian, Tibetan, and Sanskrit.

In the early 20th century, the Vaghintara script was invented for transcribing Russian words into Mongolian. However, all three scripts were short-lived.

Waiting for the bus. Behind is a Soviet Tass news agency newsphoto display.

When Mongolia was under Soviet influence, the Mongolian script was replaced by Cyrillic, an alphabet developed in the 9th century based on Greek characters and the foundation of the Russian script. Cyrillic writing cannot represent some of the sounds in spoken Mongolian. Still, the Mongolian written language today is based on Cyrillic, with some modifications. With Mongolia declaring independence from Soviet influence, there is interest in reviving the traditional script. The Mongol alphabet has 26 letters, and it is written from the top down. In 1990 the government resolved to reintroduce the Mongolian script by 1994, but this has been postponed to the year 2001.

MEDIA

The beginnings of a Mongolian language press date back to the end of the 19th century and early 20th century, when both the Soviet Union and China became more interested in increasing their influence in Mongolia. *The Mongolian Newspaper* was published in the early 1900s by Mongolian literati who wanted to liberate their country from Chinese rule. To counter its influence, China-inspired journals were distributed in Mongolia but did not find much favor. During the revolution, Mongolian revolutionaries published their own paper, the *Mongolian Truth* (*Mongolyn Ünen*), which became the journal of the Mongolian People's Revolutionary Party. Now known as *Ünen* (Truth), it is the most widely read journal with about 200,000 subscribers. There are more than 20 national newspapers.

With the greater freedom and democracy, there are now hundreds of small newspapers and other publications. Many are so small they are little more than pamphlets. There are also papers and journals produced by trade unions, the army, scientific, literary, artistic, and cultural organizations.

Mongolians have a wide choice of journals and newspapers.

The Mongolian state-run radio made its first broadcast in 1931. It broadcasts government programs as well as traditional folk music and epics, and Western classical music. Another station caters to young people, playing modern Western pop, often with English-speaking deejays. Radio Ulaanbaatar, a privately owned station, offers even more English-speaking programs and Western music. The radio is a very important source of information and entertainment, especially in rural areas. A portable radio is the herder's invaluable companion.

The programs on Ulaanbaatar TV, which started broadcasting in 1967, and other stations are largely Russian films dubbed in Mongolian, locally produced documentaries, newscasts, and sports programs, especially wrestling, which is extremely popular. National television programs are beamed to all the *aimag* capitals and to more than 50 other administrative centers. There is approximately one television set for every 20 people.

MONGOL NAMES

Mongolian names usually consist of two names. The first is the patronymic name, or the father's name, often in a possessive form; the second is the given name. So, former Prime Minister Yumjaagiyn Tsedenbal's given name is Tsedenbal. His father is Yumjaag. People are usually called by their given name. The patronymic name is rarely used in speech. When it is, it is always accompanied by the given name. When there is a title indicating a person's rank or age, it comes after the name. Mr. Tsedenbal is Tsedenbal guai ("GOO-ai").

A young girl politely offering tea to an elder, with both hands holding the bowl.

NONVERBAL LANGUAGE

Mongolians use the right hand to gesture with and to take things. When receiving a gift, food, or snuff, it is proper to do it with both hands; the right hand may be used but with the left hand touching the right elbow as if in support. Mongolians beckon someone with the fingers of the right hand, a little outstretched, palm facing down.

In the city a handshake is acceptable. In a traditional greeting between two people of different age or status, the one younger or lower in status gently supports the forearms of the other. This greeting is also used to show respect to elders during the Lunar New Year. It is impolite to point with one finger; all the fingers are used. Other taboos are crossing one's legs and kicking someone, even accidentally. An immediate apology is due. It is rude to stare directly into the eyes of an elder. Women cover their mouths in a gesture of modesty when laughing.

In greetings, an inquiry about health is added, as well as a question concerning a seasonal activity, for example, "How was the harvest?"

There are a great variety of words for grasses and animals. Mori *is a gelding.* Xiimori *is a flying, magic horse, and also means "healthy."* Morisaitai *means "fortunate" or a person who owns a good horse. The* morin khuur *is a traditional horse-head fiddle.*

ARTS

ONE MIGHT EXPECT Mongolian society to be rather underdeveloped from a cultural and artistic point of view, as it is basically a nomadic society with people remaining hardly long enough in any place to build lasting monuments or buildings.

However, Mongolians, though still largely nomadic, do have a cultural heritage going back many thousands of years. They expressed their artistic creativity in everyday articles, such as saddles and boots, and hunting tools, which they lovingly decorated.

Before writing was invented there was a very strong oral tradition, recalling history through the telling of epic stories, folktales, and songs. Professional itinerant singers traveled and performed in return for food, shelter, and money.

Later, Mongolian art and architecture served religion, as statues and paintings were created, and monasteries and temples were built.

Left: **A Mongolian saddle with decorated stirrup straps and pommel.**

Opposite: **A Mongolian musician and lute.**

BRONZE AGE CULTURE

Mongolia is said to have been inhabited from very early times, and it is also believed that humans from this part of Central Asia migrated north, crossed the landbridge, and populated North America. Stone tools dating back some 500,000 years have been found in Mongolia. The earliest evidence of some sort of art and culture comes from the Bronze Age, approximately 3000 B.C. or earlier in Mongolia.

The people, though nomadic, carved and shaped stone monuments called "reindeer stones" in the valleys, open grasslands, and hill sides, probably as markers of sacred sites or graves; these were possibly the beginnings of *ovoo*, or shaman shrines. The stones are from 3 to 13 feet (1–4 m) high and have images of celestial bodies such as the sun or the moon in the upper section, graceful deer running and jumping in the middle section, and in the bottom section, images of tools and weapons, including knives, swords, hooks, bows and quivers of arrows, and axes.

The artists of the 6th to 8th centuries had greater carving ability. They produced statues of people complete with the clothes of that period and the weapons and tools they used. This tradition continued into the 13th century.

PAINTING AND SCULPTURE

Painting in Mongolia dates back to the 8th century with the paintings of the Uighur. Later painting took on a religious significance and had Buddhist themes. The paintings were done on cloth, using mineral and vegetable dyes, and were often framed with silk. Traditionally they had red, white, or black backgrounds. Some religious paintings were appliqués created by sewing together pieces of silk and other fabric. These "silk paintings" decorated many temples and palaces. Religious paintings also hang in many homes.

Mongolian painting then took on a form called Mongol *zurag* ("ZOO-rug"), which is distinctive in almost completely filling the space, the use of certain colors, and a two-dimensional, flat style. These depict the simple life and traditions of the people. The best-known painter of this school is Balduugiyn Sharav. His most famous work is *One Day in the Life of Mongolia*. Landscape artist L. Gavaa and portrait painters O. Tsevegjav and U. Yadamsüren further developed the style of Mongol *zurag*.

Above: **A Buddhist painting.**

Opposite: **This carving of a stone man was discovered in the desolate Mongolian landscape.**

The art of reciting an epic poem is very exacting, requiring great concentration, an excellent memory, and acting and oratorical skills. Often hundreds and thousands of verses have to be learned to recite just one poem. The tradition of reciting epic poems dates back to the days when the Mongols were just a collection of tribes. One of the most ancient epics is the story of Hüüheldei Mergen Khan, a great hunter who shoots a magic deer. Another is the story of the hero Geser who is sent to earth to fight evil.

Sculpture had religious themes. Zanabazar, Mongolia's most famous sculptor and painter, created many religious statues and paintings. He learned bronze casting from the Tibetans, and his works include bronze statues of Buddhist deities, especially Tara, the deity of compassion.

LITERATURE

Mongolian heroic epics—tales of war and empire, myths of origin, histories of the great khans—were written down more than 750 years ago. The most important and earliest story ever written is *The Secret History of the Mongols*, about the origin of the greatest Mongol ever, Chinggis Khan.

After the decline of the Mongol empire, the tradition of storytelling continued into the 15th and 16th centuries, with stories about the power struggles among the many tribal princes.

The 17th century saw the rise of philosophical and didactic poetry by lamas, coinciding with the prominence of Buddhism, and this continued into the 19th century. Chinese poetry and stories were translated during the 17th to 19th centuries, including Chinese classics such as *Dream of the Red Chamber*, *Romance of the Three Kingdoms*, and *The Water Margin*.

Modern Mongol literature emerged during the revolution as writers became exposed to Western and world literature in tandem with Oriental literature, and drew inspiration from both sources. Revolutionary and nationalistic feelings were common themes of their poems, novels, and plays. Writers also translated world literature, making it possible for people to read Lu Xun, William Shakespeare, Leo Tolstoy, Alexandre Dumas, and Rabindranath Tagore in Mongolian. Modern Mongolian writers of importance are D. Natsagdorj, often described as the father of contemporary Mongolian literature, S. Buyannemeh, Ts. Damdinsüren, D. Namdag, and Z. Battulag.

SECRET HISTORY

The Secret History of the Mongols describes the origin of the Mongols, particularly the birth and rise of Chinggis Khan, the first ruler of Mongolia to unite the nomadic tribes of Central Asia. It is told in more than 30 stories and over 200 poems and songs. Also known as *The Sacred History of the Mongols*, it is part fact, part fable. A sample is given here.

In the beginning Blue-gray Wolf and Beautiful Doe came from across the sea and settled at the source of Onon River in northeast Mongolia, near Burkhan Khaldun, the "Mountain of the Shaman Spirit." Beautiful Doe gave birth to a son, Batachikhan, whose descendants pastured herds and hunted game on the slopes of the mountain.

In the 21st generation a boy was born with a clot of blood in his right fist. He was the future Chinggis Khan. His father, Yesugei the Brave, was the chief of one of the Mongol tribes. At that time there was much feuding and rivalry among the many tribes. One day, while hunting, Yesugei met a woman from another tribe and her husband and abducted her, making her his wife. Ho'elun bore him five children, four sons and a daughter. The eldest was Temujin, "blacksmith."

Temujin, at the age of 9, lost his father who was poisoned by a rival tribe, the Tatars. The family then lived on the banks of the river. The other tribes captured Temujin, afraid that he would become a leader when he came of age. They made him wear a heavy wooden yoke around his neck.

Eventually Temujin escaped and he and his family lived like outlaws on Burkhan Khaldun. He gathered followers and grew in power. In 1206, at a great assembly of all the Mongol tribes, when he was about 40 years old, Temujin was proclaimed Chinggis Khan—"strong ruler."

Two significant 19th century Mongolian writers were Noyon hutagt Ravjaa and B. Injinash. Noyon hutagt Ravjaa wrote many religious treatises, but his popularity is in the more than 400 non-religious poems and songs he composed, including Fair Wind, The Charming, *and* The Four Seasons of the Year.

B. Injinash's most famous work was the Köke Sudur *or* Blue Chronicle, *a fictional version of Mongol history upholding humanistic and patriotic ideals.*

The intricately carved and painted ceiling of a recently restored monastery.

ARCHITECTURE

Although nomadic, the Mongols built towns and villages; there is archeological evidence of more than 200 ancient towns in Mongolia. These were a combination of movable settlements and more permanent structures.

The most famous ancient city is Karakorum, built by Chinggis in 1220 on an old Uighur site on the banks of the Orhon. Construction was completed only in 1235, during Ogodei's rule. The city was divided into sectors for traders, craftsmen, artisans, administrators, and private individuals. The palace's main hall had a green enamel brick floor, and the roof tiles were green and red enamel. Around the palace were the residences of the princes and courtiers. Karakorum was destroyed by a Ming invasion in 1388, and today only one of the original four turtles believed to protect the city from floods stands a lonely guard.

There were many temples and monasteries when Mongolia was the center of the Buddhist world and influenced by both the East and the West. The famed Erdene Zuu built in 1586 was constructed on a square plan.

A brick wall topped with 108 stupas or pagodas, spaced evenly apart, enclosed it. The complex included 60 temples and 10,000 resident lamas.

DECORATIVE ARTS

Everyday objects and work tools are embellished with silver, embroidery, carvings, and appliqué work. Saddles, stirrups, and tools associated with horses are often carefully crafted and beautiful works of art. Intricate designs are carved on furniture, *ger* doors, hunting weapons, work tools, and musical instruments.

There are lavishly designed gold and silver accessories and finely embroidered pouches and cases for carrying snuff bottles, pipes, and eating sets. Traditional clothing is also enriched with finely worked gold and silver jewelry.

Traditional flint for fire-making decorated with silver.

A Kazakh folk singer in traditional costume.

SONG AND DANCE

Mongolians love music and have developed distinctive styles. There are two basic kinds of songs, the short and the long. Short songs are usually lively and tell of everyday activities, love, and nature. Long songs are more philosophical, dealing with love, the meaning of life, and the relationship between people and nature. The long song is formal and often performed at important functions, festivities, and ceremonies. They are harder to sing and some songs have as many as 20,000 lines.

A special way of singing that is not really singing but actually using the throat, tongue, mouth, and nose combined as a musical instrument, is called *khoomi* ("KHAW-me"). Professional *khoomi* singers come from certain regions where there is a strong tradition of *khoomi* singing. The Chandmani district of Hovd *aimag* in western Mongolia is the home of *khoomi*. Throat singing produces many different sounds by forcing air through the mouth and throat, and by using the tongue to form a resonant chamber in the mouth. *Khoomi* is a tradition shared with the neighboring Tuva republic, where it is known as *khoomei*. Many people have an interest in throat singing. Among them are Australians, Japanese, Americans, Canadians, Finns, and Irish.

Among the musical folk instruments are the *morin khuur* ("MAW-rin kher"), a two-stringed fiddle with a head shaped like a horse's head; the bow and string are made from the hair of a horse's tail. It creates a beautiful yet mournful sound that comes closest to expressing the deep feelings of the Mongolian heart. This instrument often accompanies the long songs telling of the beauty of the Mongolian countryside.

Some other instruments are the *shudrag* ("SHOOD rug"), a three-stringed lute with a long neck and a round wooden sound box covered with skin; the *limbe* ("LIM-beh"), a flute made of a simple, straight bamboo tube with at least eight finger holes; the *yoching* ("YAW-ching"), a board zither with two rows of 14 metal pieces stretched over a board and struck with two hammers; and the *yatag* ("YAH-tug"), a string instrument with 10 to 14 strings stretched across a long sound box.

Mongolian theater, opera, and ballet have all been influenced by the Russian forms of these arts. Russian operas are popular, but there are also Mongolian operas; the first known Mongolian opera was written by Natsagdorj. Performers were mostly trained in the Soviet Union.

Folk dancing can be seen during celebrations. The most famous dance is the *Bielgee* ("BEE-el-gee") or Dance of the Body, usually performed by a slender girl to music. The dance usually consists only of head and hand movements since this dance was originally performed in *ger* where there was little space.

LEISURE

MONGOLIANS HAVE ALWAYS SOUGHT their leisure in much the same way as they live—by being in the country, being with their horses and other animals, and hunting. Their most important and traditional leisure activities are wrestling, archery, and horse-racing. These are closely linked with the pride they feel about their history as a great and strong nation.

THREE "MANLY" SPORTS

Horse-racing, wrestling, and archery are known as the three "manly" sports, although girls and women take part in both horse-racing and archery. Practically the entire country turns out to watch competitions in these three sports during the national *Naadam* festival that takes place every July. Children learn to ride a horse almost as soon as they can walk.

"The Mongol, above all things, is not a farmer ... on the ground, he is as awkward as a duck out of water. ... The back of a pony is his real home, ... he will do wonderfully well any work which keeps him in the saddle."

—*Roy Chapman Andrews in* Across Mongolian Plains

Left: **Mongolian children playing on saddles.**

Opposite: **A family on an outing at Karakorum. The parents are in traditional** *del* **and the children in modern dress.**

Mongolians ride standing nearly upright in short stirrups. An urgha *("OOR-ga"), a willow or bamboo pole about 30 feet (9 m) long with a rope attached to the tip, is used to lasso animals.*

Riding skill is necessary in a pastoral and nomadic society, with families moving with the seasons. Mongolians do not learn riding for sport but as a necessary skill. Practically every Mongolian knows how to ride a horse, and they are said to be excellent equestrians.

Mongolian boys are also taught to wrestle from an early age. The most promising are trained in special camps. They learn all the classic moves and throws, the correct wrestler's stance (supposed to be a combination of the posture of a lion and the outspread wings of a bird in flight), and how to do the victorious "eagle dance."

Archery, the third "manly sport," is practiced by both men and women, using the same type of equipment and technique. The Mongolian bow is

a double-curved bow, made of horn, sinew, bark, and wood. The arrowhead is made of bone. The string is drawn back with the aid of a thumb ring made of leather.

OTHER TRADITIONAL GAMES

The game of "shooting bones" has been around since the time of Chinggis Khan. It is played with the anklebone of a lamb. Each side of the bone has a name—horse, camel, goat, and sheep. Sets of eight or 12 bones are "shot" at a target, two at a time, with the aid of a special plank. The winner is the one with the greatest number of bones at the end of the game.

"Catching horses" is another popular pastime. Boys in one group separate a wild horse from the rest of the herd, then chase it back at high speed. Another group of boys waits for the horse to gallop by and tries to lasso it. This game develops a very important skill for Mongolian boys.

HUNTING

Mongolians love hunting, which for them has a practical purpose. They shoot various animals such as deer, rabbit, and marmot for their meat, pelt, and other valuable parts and kill animals that prey on livestock. Hunting used to be carried out with spears or bows and arrows; traps and guns have largely taken their place.

Wolves are a favorite target because they attack livestock, their pelts bring a good price, and their meat is valued for its medicinal qualities. Marmots are also a common target almost everywhere on the steppes.

Above: **A Kazakh hunter with his hunting eagle.**

Opposite: **A young boy riding bareback.**

Mongolian herders allow their horses to roam freely, making them semiwild. They have to corral, lasso, and break these horses in again to use them.

Young people listening to a rock band.

LEISURE IN THE CITY

Going to the movies is increasingly popular, particularly among the young. Most of the films used to be from the Soviet Union and East European countries, but Hollywood films have an increasing hold on movie-goers. American westerns are very popular, possibly because of the scenes of wide-open spaces and horses. Television and radio help to occupy the long hours especially during the winter.

Young Mongolians love listening to Western popular music, including jazz and rock. There are also a number of homegrown Mongolia rock and even heavy metal groups.

Going window-shopping is an increasing leisure activity especially in the towns.

There are many recreational spas at hot springs with waters that have health and curative effects. The government has built holiday camps for workers to go on vacations.

Naturally, the outdoors is very important even for those who live in cities, who like to go to the countryside to visit friends and relatives. Those who can afford it retreat to country *ger* or small cabins in the summer.

MODERN SPORTS

Mongolians are very sports-oriented as they have a nomadic tradition that keeps them outdoors and physically active. Football, basketball, volleyball, soccer, and gymnastics are popular. Ulaanbaatar has a soccer stadium and an indoor coliseum. Motorcycle racing and bicycling, hang gliding, and mountain climbing have many enthusiasts. Skiing and ice skating on frozen rivers and lakes are extremely popular winter sports.

Sports are nurtured in schools as an important part of the curriculum. This importance is reflected in the National Games, a nationwide competition of 17 winter and summer sports organized by the country's sports clubs and associations.

A young Mongolian film industry has developed. One popular film, actually set and filmed in Inner Mongolia, is called Urgha. It takes a funny and human look at Mongolian life and the conflict of cultures.

MONGOLIAN CHESS

The game of chess is a very old and traditional pastime and is extremely popular, as is checkers, in Mongolia. Mongolian chess is played on a chessboard similar to the Western chessboard but the game pieces are different, reflecting Mongolia's pastoral and nomadic lifestyle. The king, pawn, knight, castle, bishop, and queen are replaced by the khan, boy, horse, cart, camel, and lion or dog.

Mongolians have also done well in international competitions. Their athletes take part in the Asian Games, the Olympic Games, and various world championships. They have done very well in freestyle wrestling, winning five silvers and three bronzes in the Olympic Games in the 20-year period from 1968 to 1988.

FOLKTALES

The telling of folktales is an old and important tradition. Besides the entertainment provided, folktales communicate traditions and values from

HOW THE CAMEL LOST ITS ANTLERS AND ITS TAIL

Once upon a time, the camel had beautiful antlers on its head and a long, luxurious tail. The deer, on the other hand, had a bald head and the horse, a thin and bedraggled tail. Both the deer and the horse envied the camel for its wonderful good looks.

One day, when the camel went down to the water to drink, it met the deer. "Could I borrow your antlers for a day?" the deer asked the camel. "There is a big celebration tonight and I am ashamed of going with my bald head." The camel, being generous, agreed, on condition that the deer would come to the water's edge the next day and return the antlers.

As the happy deer went on its way, holding its head up high to show off the antlers it had just gained, it met the horse. "Where did you get those antlers?" asked the horse. The deer told the horse. The horse thought this would be an excellent chance to fool the camel and get its lovely tail. The horse ran down to the water and to its delight saw the camel still standing there. Using the same story as the deer, the horse persuaded the camel to part with its tail.

The next morning, the camel went back to the water's edge again to look for the deer and the horse and get back its possessions. But, of course, they did not appear. To this day, when the camel takes a drink, it will have a few sips, then look up and gaze out at the steppes, hoping to catch sight of the deer and the horse, but it never does.

Mongolians use the word *genin* ("GEN-in") to describe the camel and the same word to describe a person who is too generous for his own good.

one generation to the next. Storytellers are the older folk, but there are also professional storytellers who tell a story for some money, food, and shelter, and often accompany their stories with songs.

Many folktales have animals with human qualities as the main characters. The snake is often a bad character; so is the hedgehog, though not as bad as the snake. The lion, dragon, elephant, and the mythical *garuda* ("ga-ROO-da") are strong animals with good attributes. The horse is often magical and intelligent, capable of incredible feats and able to fly. Although a man may be the hero in the story, it is the horse that often grabs the limelight as the real hero, giving the rider advice, warning of dangers, and foretelling events to come. The camel is thought of as kind and generous and often too trusting of others.

Characters depicting ordinary, simple folk with qualities like honesty, wisdom, and kindness, who triumph over evil, greed, and injustice of all kinds, include such characters as the clever Badarchin, a wandering lama; the storyteller Dalan Hudalch; and the witty Tsartsan Namjil.

THE MONGOLIAN CIRCUS

Although it emerged only in the 1930s, the circus is a unique form of art in Mongolia and a direct result of Soviet influence. Following a tour by a Soviet circus troupe in 1931, the first group of Mongolian circus artistes was sent to the Soviet Union for training.

In the 70 years it has been in existence, the Mongolian circus has performed all over the world. A specialty of the circus is contortionism, in which artistes perform complicated contorted postures, while in precarious balancing positions. It has become a highlight of the Mongolian circus. Circus acts are sometimes performed in the open air in the countryside.

FESTIVALS

BEFORE THE REVOLUTION, many festivals in Mongolia were connected with days of religious significance. Celebrations were also held to mark important events such as weddings. After the revolution, however, the state's efforts to stamp out religion led to most holidays becoming a celebration of socialist and state objectives, such as the solidarity of workers.

Only two traditional celebrations, New Year's Day and *Naadam*, have survived. Even then, *Naadam*, the biggest and most popular celebration of the year, has been given a political significance; it is now held on July 11 and 12 to celebrate the people's revolution.

There are annual festivals like the Golden Autumn Music Festival and the Snowdrop Music Festival for Children, and festivals celebrated only every five years like the International Circus Festival and National Amateur Folklore Art Festival.

Each year in the 12-year lunar cycle is named after an animal, beginning with the year of the rat, followed by those of the ox, tiger, rabbit, dragon, snake, horse, sheep or goat, monkey, cockerel, dog, and pig. These years have alternating male and female characteristics. The male (called "hard" years) are the rat, tiger, dragon, horse, monkey, and dog years. The rest are female, or "easy," years.

Left: **Women in** *del* **at the National Day** *Naadam* **Parade.**

Opposite: **A young contestant at a horse race, the** *Soyombo* **symbol on her cap for good luck.**

Festivities are held for special events such as when a child is born or a new *ger* erected, a child's first haircut, the first day of making *airag* and new felt, and special days for herdsmen, camel breeders, and milkmaids.

NEW YEAR'S DAY

The exact day for the start of a new year depends on the lunar calendar, but it usually falls between the end of January and early February. New Year's Day is known as "White Moon" or "White Month."

On New Year's Eve the family gathers at the home of the eldest member for a celebratory meal. On New Year's Day, milk and *airag* are offered to

On a hill top, a retired farm manager burns incense on New Year's Day while his grandson watches.

the spirit of the sky and each family member has to walk in the direction specified by a book of omens. Family members then greet each other with good wishes. The oldest member of the family is the first to be greeted. Once the greetings are over the rest of the day is spent in eating, drinking, and socializing. A festive table is usually set up in each home. People go from house to house visiting family and friends.

Activities such as horse races, wrestling, and other competitions are organized by local community leaders as part of the New Year celebrations.

NAADAM

Naadam is the best-known festival and biggest event of the year. It marks the high point of the summer when people travel hundreds of miles across the country to a common meeting ground where they can celebrate with sports and feasting. Smaller *Naadam* festivals may be held to celebrate religious and other occasions. Since 1922 the biggest *Naadam* occurs in Ulaanbaatar to celebrate Mongolia's National Day.

For days before the big *Naadam*, people ride in on their horses—families in trucks and on horse-drawn wooden carts—and set up their *ger* just outside the city. The temporary city grows as people gather and wait for the entertainment and festivities to begin.

Naadam is a sports-oriented festival and the most exciting events are the contests in wrestling, archery, and horse-riding.

Hundreds of wrestlers come from all over the country to test their strength and skill against each other. The event takes place in the national stadium. There are no weight categories or age limits as in international wrestling competitions, but the wrestlers are all big and muscular men. Traditionally, either 1,024 or 512 wrestlers take part in the contest, which lasts throughout the two or three days of the *Naadam* festival because there are so many wrestling contestants.

Participants in horse-riding are boys and girls 5 to 12 years old. Races are run over distances from 10 to 20 miles (16 to 32 km). The distance is set by the horse's age, not the child's. The children often ride bareback, being skilled riders and tacticians. They know how to conserve the horse's energy to last the distance and to have that extra spurt near the finishing line.

Before the race begins, the riders go three times around the starting point, giving an ancient war cry. They wear bright and colorful clothes with symbols of good luck on their backs. The course takes them once around the stadium, then out into the country where they have to negotiate numerous obstacles such as rivers and hills.

The winning riders do laps of honor around the stadium and ride up to the grandstand to receive the ceremonial bowls of *airag* of which they drink a little, pouring the rest on the horses. Honor is also paid to the less fortunate losers. They are led up to the grandstand together with their mounts, while the spectators shout words of encouragement and appreciation for their efforts, and a special chant is said in their honor.

Archery, though called a "manly" sport, also has women participants. The archers are dressed in *del* and traditional pointed hats. Both men and

Above: **Young riders neck and neck at the finishing line in a horse-racing contest.**

Opposite: **An experienced archer demonstrates his skill.**

women use the same kind of bow and shooting technique. When a target is hit, a group of judges sing a short ceremonial song of praise. The winner of the archery contest is declared "sharpshooter."

RELIGIOUS MASKED DANCE FESTIVAL

The religious masked dance festival was performed in big monasteries in ancient times. It originated in India and spread to Tibet. From there, it was brought to Mongolia in the 16th century. Part dance and part mystery play, the masked dance was based on Buddhist mythology. It formed part of Buddhist rites.

The masks were made from papier-mâché and decorated with precious stones, metals, and coral. They were vividly colored in red, black, yellow, white, and blue, and were bigger than life-size so they could be seen clearly and appreciated by the audience. The masks depicted Buddhist deities such as the fierce protector gods, and Yama, the Lord of Death. The Mongolian costumes, masks, and sets were different from those in Tibet.

The dances frequently told of the triumph of good over evil, with characters such as the funny White Old Man, a buffoon, the Dark Old Man in his black mask and white fangs, and Garuda, the mountain god; these were elements of witchcraft and shamanism.

From the 16th to the 19th centuries each of the 700 major monasteries staged a big performance once a year. The last was held in Ulaanbaatar in the late 1930s. After that the communist suppression of Buddhism began.

HAIR-CUTTING CEREMONY

The hair-cutting ceremony occurs when a child is 3 to 5 years old and believed to have passed the dangers of infancy. It is an old nomadic tradition that is celebrated with great joy. Hair cutting normally takes place in the fall.

Traditionally the day is chosen by a lama. Days beforehand, the preparation of festive food begins, and on the big day the festive table is laden with food and drink.

The child goes from guest to guest with a pair of scissors and a ceremonial blue silk bag. Each person cuts off a little lock of hair, puts it in the bag, and gives the child a present or gift of money. Throughout the ceremony everyone eats, drinks, and talks.

FOOD

MONGOLIANS EAT MAINLY MEAT (the fatter the better) and dairy products. Both are readily available from the domestic animals they raise—camels, cattle, goats, and sheep. One is unlikely to meet a Mongolian vegetarian unless he happens to be a Buddhist monk. The short growing season makes the growing of vegetables a difficult task. Vegetable farming was left to the Chinese, and it was only after the revolution that the government introduced farming into the economy.

Mongolians eat three regular meals a day. Breakfast and lunch usually consist of dairy foods, and sometimes meat. Meat is usually present at the evening meal. Tea is drunk throughout the day. The whole family gathers for dinner, usually eating boiled mutton, a favorite dish, and noodle soup.

Eating utensils depend on the food. Mongolians use chopsticks for noodles, spoons for vegetables and rice, and knives for cutting meat. Hardly any other spice except salt is used for seasoning.

"Mongolians, we quickly learned, love meat and fat, and in fact consider meat without fat unappetizing and inadequate. Once, when we were trying to buy meat ... a young man we knew brought us a leg of mutton but refused payment because he said the meat wasn't good quality. It was lean, and taking money would be like cheating us."

—M.C. Goldstein and
C.M. Beall in
The Changing World of
Mongolia's Nomads

Left: **Sausages and vegetables for a meal.**

Opposite: **Women frying noodles with mutton.**

MUTTON IS THE BEST

Mongolians enjoy beef and mutton, especially the latter. Horsemeat is popular among the Kazakhs in the west. Besides the meat of their domestic animals, Mongolians also like eating marmots, rabbit, deer, and wild boar.

Mutton is prepared by cutting it into joints and smaller pieces, then boiled or made into a stew. Very little of the sheep is wasted. Besides the meat, the lungs, heart, stomach, intestines, liver, and blood are boiled and eaten. Meat that cannot be used up is dried and preserved.

A national dish, *buuz* ("BUHZ"), is a dumpling filled with chopped mutton. *Khuurshuur* ("KHER-sher") is a fried pancake made of flour and mutton. Sheep's blood and intestines are the chief ingredients of a sausage-like dish. Barbecued mutton is called *shorlog* ("SHOR-log"). *Khorkhog* ("KHOR-kohg") is usually cooked on special occasions like festivals. A goat or sheep is killed and placed on hot coals, and hot rocks are put inside the carcass so that it is cooked evenly from the inside out.

Animal fat is relished. Chunks of fat often float in the stews. The Mongolian fat-tailed sheep, a special breed, has a tail usually cooked as a delicacy, and so fatty it weighs more than 20 pounds (9 kg).

Only recently have onions, potatoes, and cabbage appeared in the diet. People in the countryside, especially the less affluent, eat mainly pickled vegetables rather than fresh vegetables and fruit.

The staple food is a soft wheat flour pastry, rolled out and formed into shapes, then deep-fried. Large amounts of this are eaten at mealtimes with meat, cheeses, and tea. Rice, noodles and bread are also staples. Fish and chicken are not common items in the Mongolian diet.

"WHITE FOOD"

Dairy products from camels, mares, sheep, goats, and cows are called "white food," the second most important food.

Women milk the animals. The milk is boiled and set aside; the skin is skimmed off and dried slightly to make a soft, creamy, pancake-like food, a delicacy eaten on its own or spread on pastries. The boiled milk is put into a leather bag, standard equipment found in every *ger,* and left to ferment. It is stirred with a long wooden paddle every day, churning the

Above: **Sour cottage cheese and a dry, sweet curd pressed into blocks can often be seen drying on the *ger* tops.**

Opposite: **Making sausages.**

Boiling and storing milk.

The quality of tea is very poor. Bits of tea leaves, twigs, and other impurities are pressed into bricks for easy storage and transport. The tea bricks are so hard that small chunks have to be chipped off with a knife or hammer.

milk into butter, which is removed. The remaining milk or buttermilk is used to make *arkhi* ("AHR-khee"), an alcoholic drink.

All these dairy products are made in the summer and fall. Many are dried and keep well for months, always available for eating during the winter months. Despite consuming huge quantities of dairy products and animal fat, studies have not discovered any unusually high levels of cholesterol among the population.

MILK-TEA

Mongolians drink tea at meals and in between. There is usually a big pot of tea in the *ger* always ready. Milk-tea is made by boiling tea leaves in water and adding some milk, butter, and salt gradually to the mixture. It is stirred by scooping it with a ladle and pouring it back into the pot from some height. Sometimes when milk is not available, herders make the tea with boiled salted water, and leave it to boil for a while.

RECIPE FOR *BUUZ*

minced lamb, which should be fatty   salt
pepper and salt to taste   plain flour
paprika, marjoram, cumin (optional)   water

Mix lamb with pepper, salt, and a sprinkle of any of the optional spices.

Add a dash of salt to flour and a little water at a time, kneading till you get a firm dough. Roll out the dough to an eighth of an inch (3 mm) thick. Use a cutter or a tumbler to cut out circles of dough 4–6 inches (10–15 cm) in diameter.

Put a little minced lamb in the center of each circle. Bring up the edges of the dough so that it forms a ball in your hand. Pinch the edges of the dough together, leaving a little gap open at the top.

Place the balls in a steamer. Steam until the meat is cooked and *buuz* is ready to serve.

For *khuurshuur*, use the same ingredients, but put the minced lamb in one half of the circle and flip the other half over it. Pinch the edges together. Fry the pastry until light brown and crisp.

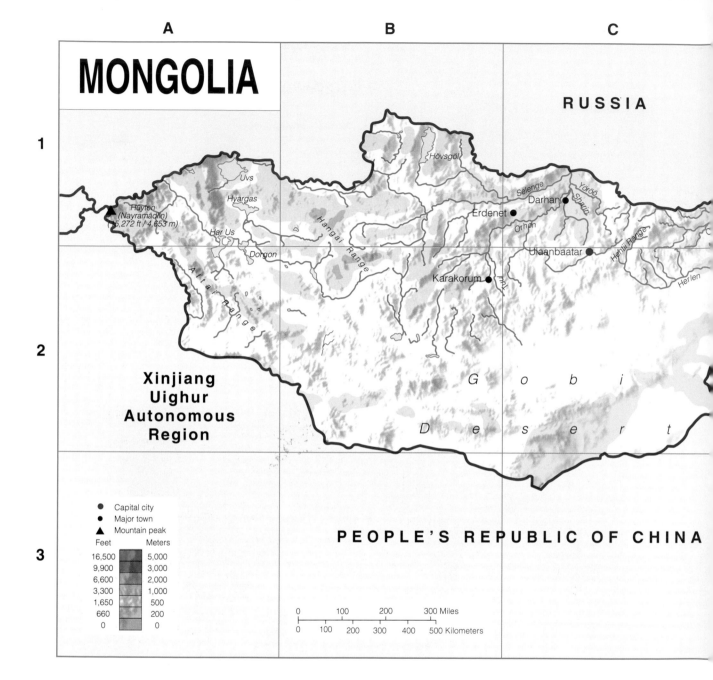

MONGOLIA

A **B** **C**

1

2

3

RUSSIA

Hövsgöl

Uvs

Hyargas

Hüyten
(Nayramadlin)
(15,272 ft / 4,653 m)

Har Us

Dorgon

Selenge

Darhan

Erdenet

Orhon

Yöröö

Shuu

Hentii Range

Ulaanbaatar

Herlen

Karakorum

Tuul

Hangai Range

Altai Range

Xinjiang Uighur Autonomous Region

G o b i

D e s e r t

PEOPLE'S REPUBLIC OF CHINA

● Capital city
● Major town
▲ Mountain peak

Feet	Meters
16,500	5,000
9,900	3,000
6,600	2,000
3,300	1,000
1,650	500
660	200
0	0

0   100   200   300 Miles

0   100   200   300   400   500 Kilometers

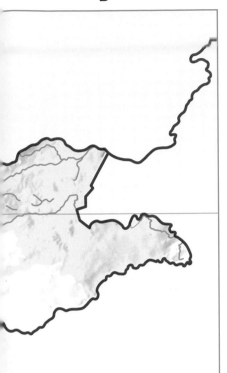

N

Altai Range, A2

Darhan, C1

Dorgon (lake), A2

Erdenet, C1

Gobi Desert, B2–C2

Hangai Range,
   B1–B2

Har Us (lake),
   A1–A2

Hentii Range,
   C1–C2

Herlen (river),
   C2–D2

Hövsgöl (lake), B1

Hüyten
   (mountain), A1

Hyargas (lake), A1

Karakorum, B2

Onon (river), C1

Orhon (river), C1

People's Republic of
   China, B3

Russia, C1

Selenge (river), C1

Sharin (river), C1

Tuul (river), C2

Ulaanbaatar, C2

Uvs (lake), A1

Xinjiang Uighur
   Autonomous
   Region, A2

Yöröö (river), C1

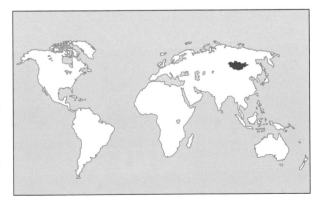

QUICK NOTES

LAND AREA
604,000 square miles (1,565,000 square km)

POPULATION
2.3 million

CAPITAL
Ulaanbaatar

NATIONAL SYMBOL
Soyombo, symbol of sovereignty and independence.

STATE EMBLEM
A circle with a white lotus at its base. The background color, blue, symbolizes the eternal blue sky. In the center is the Precious Steed and the Golden *Soyombo.* Above is the Wish-granting Jewel, a symbol of the past, present, and future. In the lower part the Wheel entwined with the Ceremonial Silk Scarf expresses reverence, respect, and continued prosperity. The mountain symbolizes Mother Earth.

NATIONAL FLAG
A rectangle divided vertically into three equal portions, a blue rectangle symbolizing the eternal blue sky between two red rectangles symbolizing progress and prosperity. The *soyombo* symbol is in the left red rectangle.

MAJOR RIVERS
Orhon, Herlen, Selenge, Tuul

MAJOR LAKES
Uvs, Hövsgöl, Har Us

HIGHEST POINT
Hüyten (15,272 feet/4,653 m)

OFFICIAL LANGUAGE
Khalkha Mongol

MAJOR RELIGION
Buddhism

CURRENCY
Monetary unit, the *tögrög*, equal to 100 *möngö.* US$1 = 750 *tögrög*

MAIN EXPORTS
Copper, molybdenum, fluorspar, cashmere, wool, hides, and skins

IMPORTANT HOLIDAYS
New Year's Day, January 1; Lunar New Year, late January or early February; Mother and Child Day, June 1; National Day, July 11–13

LEADERS IN POLITICS
Chinggis Khan (1167–1227), empire builder; Gombodorji Zanabazar (1635–1723), reincarnate lama; Damdin Sukhebaatar (1893–1923), revolutionary leader

LEADERS IN LITERATURE
Ts. Dambadorj (1900–1934), S. Buyannemeh (1902–1936), Dashdorjin Natsagdorj (1906–1937), Z. Battulag (1919–1983), Ts. Damdinsüren (1928–1986)

LEADERS IN ART
G. Zanabazar (1635–1723), Balduugiyn Sharav (1869–1939)

GLOSSARY

aimag ("AI-mug")
Provinces or political subdivisions, of which there are 18 in Mongolia.

airag ("AI-rug")
Fermented mare's milk.

arkhi ("AHR-khee")
Alcoholic drink distilled from cow's milk.

Bielgee ("BEE-el-gee")
Mongolian dance performed by a girl.

buuz ("BUHZ")
Fried dumpling, a pastry filled with mutton.

del ("DEHL")
Mongolian traditional dress.

ger ("GUHR")
Tent dwelling.

khalkha ("HAL-ha")
Shield or alliance. The Khalka are a nomadic people living in eastern and central Mongolia.

khoomi ("KHAW-me")
Throat singing.

Lama
Buddhist monk.

morin khuur ("MAW-rin kher")
Two-stringed Mongolian fiddle with a head shaped like a horse's head.

örtöö ("OOR-taw")
Courier system of horseriders.

ovoo ("AW-waw")
Mound of rocks to honor the gods and spirits.

shudrag ("SHOOD-rug")
Three-stringed Mongolian lute.

Silk Road
An ancient trade route linking China and imperial Rome, named after the silk carried on it. Caravans generally met on the road and traded goods.

Soyombo ("SOH-yom-bo")
Mongolian symbol on the national flag consisting of a star, a flame, a sun, a crescent moon, two intertwined fish, rectangles, and triangles.

State Great Hural
The Mongolian parliament.

Tengri ("TENG-ri")
The Supreme or Eternal Sky God.

tögrög ("TOOG-roog")
Mongolian currency.

yoching ("YAW-ching")
Mongolian zither with metal pieces stretched on a board, struck with two hammers.

zurag ("ZOO-rug")
A two-dimensional painting style in Mongolia that uses distinctive colors.

BIBLIOGRAPHY

Avery, Martha. *Women of Mongolia*. Boulder, Colorado: Asian Art & Archaeology, 1996.

Brill, Marlene Targ. *Enchantment of the World: Mongolia*. Chicago: Children's Press, 1992.

Goldstein, Melvyn C. & Cynthia M. Beall. *The Changing World of Mongolia's Nomads*. Los Angeles: University of California Press, 1994.

Major, John S. *The Land and People of Mongolia*. New York: J.B. Lippincott, 1990.

Middleton, Nick. *The Last Disco in Outer Mongolia*. London: Sinclair-Stevenson Ltd, 1992.

Severin, Tim. *In Search of Genghis Khan*. London: Arrow Books, 1991.

INDEX

INDEX

INDEX

4/99